PASSIVE INCOME INV

A beginner's guide on financial freedom with secrets, ideas and blueprint. Investing and make money online with Blogging, Dropshipping, ecommerce and Affiliate Marketing

Table of Contents

INTRODUCTION

Unequivocally, I can vehemently say that earning passive income is interesting and sweet. It has the capacity of transmitting you from the poverty level to being very rich. Especially when you passively make your earnings online. Trust me, the world has become a digital motherboard where everyone needs to tap current from. It has been said that we are in the digital age and we all need to connect to this online matter.

A lot of people around you earn from online platforms, so why can't you? Or do you feel you are rich enough? But even if you are rich enough, Bill Gates still looks for money, so why can't you?

This book has been written to put you through some means through which you can invest online and get your passive income. As you may have known, the online world doesn't require you to put on your suit and neatly polished shoes and set out for work. You could work even if you are in the loo. You could work and earn thousands of US dollar right from the comfort of your room. The idea is that you sit in your room, work right from there and smile to the bank to cash out.

This is not to say that earning money online is a get rich quick scheme or something, it only means you put in some efforts and dedication. So, if you are the kind of person whose interest doesn't wane easily and you are dedicated to making, you need to try the methods recommended in this book.

There are a lot of methods to make money online. There are freelancing, writing, voice over making, video editing, vlogging, et cetera. However, for the purpose of this book, we will be discussing the following only:

1. Blogging
2. Drop shipping
3. E-commerce
4. Affiliate Marketing, among others

Stay connected and you can be assured of getting the best out of this book. Enjoy....

BLOGGING

Blogging has to do with creating a website that has contents for the consumption of a target audience. Since this is a platform to reach people, you may earn money through advertising to your audience, you could also sell products to them, blogging has a lot of ways through which you can make money from.

What Is Blog and Its Origin?

Goodbye journals and hello blogging. This is now the common trend of expressing one's opinion about anything under the sun—blogging. But what is really a blog and where it came from?

Blog is actually coined from the word "weblog," which was shortened to "blog." A blog may refer to the entire website owned by a certain group or person where all the entries can be read and commented. The word "blog" can also be used as a verb, meaning, to add and maintain entries or contents to a blog site. The word may have many uses but it only requires one thing for a certain entry or website to qualify as a blog. That is, it should be shared, maintained, and used through the Internet. If not, a certain entry will never be a blog. People may write similar contents with blogs and save it in their computer. But that content will remain as a document or file and not a blog unless the content will be published online. That's the time that the content or the site can be considered as a blog.

The idea of blogging actually came in the late 80s when some people learned how to post contents using a certain network. The use of Internet was not wide then, so, the "blogging" of that time was never on the news. It was only in the late 90s when the word "weblog" was used and the word "blog" came into existence.

Due to the increasing demand for blog sites then, some groups decided to create blog hosting sites. This move is owed for the boost of blogging market that people have today.

Common Mistakes on a Blog Website

Blog website is considered as the home of all the blog entries. Being that, the layout of it should be well-planned to attract more readers. Not only that, it should be informative enough to gain the trust of the readers. However, due to the popularity of blogs as a way to earn income, anyone just want to create their own blog websites without knowing anything what should and should not be done, leading them to do one of the common mistakes in making a blog website.

One of the usual mistakes that blogger do when creating a blog website is not putting enough information about the author. If company websites have their "about us" page, then the blogger should have his "about me" page. This should discuss who is the owner of the blog website and what makes him credible in all the opinions he has written. Another mistake most people do is not putting the author's photo. Some say that photos are not that important. But if the goal is to have personal impression and to connect more effectively with readers, then having photos is important.

Some bloggers also create non-descriptive titles on their posts. The title should say about the gist of the blog and not just to make a sense of surprise for the reader. Also, the links provided by some bloggers are sometimes anonymous. They do not label where the links will lead the reader. Another mistake is that some bloggers only use the calendars as their navigation. This should not be the case since the blog entries themselves can be used to navigate to other related articles. This can be done through linking or suggesting to readers. By avoiding these common mistakes, bloggers can certainly create better blog websites that readers will appreciate more.

How to Start a Blog?

There might be thousands of blog locales previously existing in the Internet today. Maybe, there are presently millions of blog sections everywhere throughout the world. This enormous number just demonstrates the fame of blogging far and wide making everybody need to start their very own blog website. Be that as it may, not every person has the thought on how to start a blog.

Beginning a blog is now simpler thought about to beginning a blog a couple of years back. Blogging is made simpler and less expensive now with the free destinations and free tools that a possibility blogger can utilize. To start a blog, it is significant to first set up a blog site. Making a blog site doesn't require to purchase another area name. There are currently blog facilitating locales like blogger and Wordpress giving free site to the individual. These additionally have their own tools like word processing tools, CSS and HTML editors, and abilities to embed recordings, pictures, and connections.

Blog facilitating destinations additionally offer various design styles and topics that can be utilized for nothing. On the off chance that any of the accessible subjects sometimes fall short for the taste of the individual, he can download free topics from other blog sites. Altering the HTML is likewise conceivable with other blog facilitating locales making the design and subject of the blog website increasingly customized.

There are additionally tools and gadgets that can be included the blog website like schedule, visitor counter, word counter, and other fun stuffs. Some blog destinations can likewise buy in to different sites for better third party referencing and better blog content.

The Internet offers more alternatives for the individual. He simply needs to investigate all of these and be progressively innovative.

Tips on how to make a Blog

There are a great deal of individuals who have the heart recorded as a hard copy yet have not yet discovered the correct road to write their considerations and thoughts. There are the individuals who have effectively discovered the ideal road however have not yet understood the true abilities of the tool. Making a blog is a significant extremely basic and simple procedure to complete. While to some this may look like confused like tackling a logarithmic issue, yet by and large of individuals who have attempted web logging would state the otherwise. The following are some of the valuable tips that one can use in making a web log:

a. Ensure that you know where your aptitudes and information lie. There are a ton of web lumberjacks who have differing musings in their mind that now and again they are not capable to thought of one strong thought to make. Ensure that you decongest your psyche with the topics that you need to compose. Compose the things that are driving too much enthusiasm for you.

b. Ensure that you are capable to make a draft before making a last web log article. Drafting is consistently advised earlier to having a last structure in light of the fact that the draft permits you to re-make and re-establish your contemplations and thoughts.

c. Pick the best web log application tool. You can look over utilizing the BlogSpot website or the Wordpress application while making your web log. These two known tools are giving exceptionally ground-breaking highlights that can assist you with kicking off your web logging vocation.

Blogging as a means to generate more Money

Web logging utilized to be an outsider term to by and large a ton of individuals. In any case, as the Internet has quick turning into the mode of every day exchanges for individuals, this term has step by step earned acknowledgment from individuals. From the start, web logging has been regarded as a structure of communicating somebody's suppositions – an ideal road to fundamentally discharge your contemplations and feelings and experiences. At that point, at one point, it has gotten the medium utilized by individuals to impel ideas and in the long run a structure of composing to impact the musings of others.

As the web logging industry become basically dynamic, it has opened new entryways of open doors for others.

What utilized to be a structure of past time currently has become a more grounded methods to win a living and produce a continuing mechanism. Through blogging, the blogger can draw in advertisers to utilize their blog webpage as the road to advance and advertise their items. Consequently, the blogger is paid for the space that the advertisement has utilized on the blog webpage. The activity may come to be repetitive, from the start, however subsequent to having established a superior page positioning and fame, things will come simply simple for the web loggers.

What are the "To-Do-Lists" on a Blog?

Prior to deciding the kind of web log that you are going to create and build, there are a few to-do-lists that you may want to check out first. These to-do-lists can greatly help you in attaining a well-structured and well-written web log that could attract more and more potential viewers and eventually increase strongly your potential to get a higher page rank. Below are some of the to-do-lists that you may want to take into account to:

a. Choose appropriately the type of skin and design for the web log. The design and the skin reflect your bare personality as a person and as a web logger. Your readers are not able to see you much more get to know you in person. Every little detail that you put onto your web log is a manifestation of your character and personality.

b. Choose the kind of topic that you put as a content on your web log. Basically choosing a topic or content has only two bases: the one that you are interested with and the one that interests your prospective readers. It is best that you opt at what interests you because you are able to write well and good when you know that what you are expressing are the ideas and concepts that bear passion to you. The one that interests your prospective clients should only be secondary as this may bring difficulty in the duration of writing the whole content.

c. Choose a date and time when you do periodic maintenance on your web log site. This will give you ample time to reflect on what sort of things you may want to include on your maintenance and updating period.

The Significance of a Blog Traffic

In the Internet world, traffic is a synonymous term that blends with all aspects of it. Traffic is such a huge word that every Internet people must understand and comprehend with ease. Most online business people are well-acquainted with the term traffic as their business activities basically revolve around how they can be able to generate more traffic for their site.

Just any online business person, web loggers are also concerned about how well their web log is doing in terms of generated traffic. Traffic for web loggers bears significance because of the following reasons:

a. More traffic means higher page ranking. Higher page ranking means established identity as a robust and trusted web log site. In the end, these and all boil down to one thing – more income to generate.

b. More traffic can boost your confidence about what you are pouring into your web log is something that is well appreciated thus create an appeal and interest to potential readers. This is more of a psyche thing for the web logger.

c. More traffic is significant in ensuring that what you put onto your web log is something that passes the taste and standards of your potential readers and the standards of the search engine.

Although, generally speaking, traffic spells more income for the web logger, significantly it bears importance on how the person perceives about what he writes and what he includes on his web log content. Having said this, the important aspect that it plays is more on how it can uplift the mental and esteem sides of the person writing the web log.

The Benefits of Free Blog Hosting

Your web log regardless of the type of contents and range of audience that it targets requires that it gets hosted by a web log server. The purpose of the blog hosting is to make sure that your web log gets the right avenue to have it exposed and essentially be seen by the potential clients. There are hosting domains that are offering a free service that provides premium features.

However, since most of the jump starters in web logging are not yet attaining an established status in the web logging industry, they opt at having free blog hosting instead.

Free blog hosting is generally beneficial to web loggers. It is given that when you choose at having a free blog hosting, you are not tied up with any commitment with the domain hosting thus eliminate the burden of having to think about your monthly or annual fee to your domain hosting site. Specifically, the ones written below are the sound benefits of a free blog hosting:

a. You are not pressured to think about the time frame of getting your return of investment because you do not a monthly obligation to settle.

b. You are capable of creating a new web log without having to think about whether the other web log is generating income or not. The free blog hosting site does not limit you in creating a single web log.

c. Free blog hosting seemingly has similar features to that of premium, although there are quite a few dynamic features that fee-based hosting offer to the web log owner. But generally of the basic features that are present on the fee-based are similarly present with the free hosting.

Blogging Software: Your Tool To Right Blogging

To get yourself equipped with blogging tools like blogging software is the secret of successfully setting up and maintaining your fledgling weblog. Once you were able to set-up your site using the most appropriate blogging software you wouldn't encounter any trouble along the way, in this case, the maintenance of your blog.

Blog itself is considered as the trendiest and newest publishing tool in the mainstream media. In fact, blogs not just a popular tool in publishing your thoughts and ideas, it is also becoming the forefront in business and marketing tools. Businesses are transforming, and they are now becoming technologically-inclined and their attitude towards blogs is highly optimistic. They used blogs as their secret weapon in building a long-lasting relationship with their customers through information sharing and corporate culture knowledge.

The success of businesses that employ blogs, as one of their marketing tools, depends on the blogging software that they will utilize. Ending up with the right software means a quicker start and a smooth processing ahead of you. And for the record, there are two types of blog software intended for somebody who wishes to get his works published. The first kind is called the hosted blog software wherein all the data that gets published are stored in the software of the host company. The other type is called the independent blog software wherein the software should be downloaded first from the company and then get installed on a web server.

Whichever type of blogging software suits your needs you are already in the safe position since you were able to make a good head start.

Popular Blogs Due to Market, Politics, Products, and Entertainment Commentaries

Something becomes popular because it provides overwhelming information; the same thing goes to recognizing popular blogs. Blogs become popular because the author mainly addresses issues concerning the market, politics, products, and entertainment matters. And behind every blog's popularity is definitely a high-paying adsense keywords.

In this case, let us have the top 10 most popular blogs that were rated according to the authority and influences that the blog possesses.

1. The Breaking News and Opinion on the Huffington Post which typically adheres to political issues and world news.

2. The TechCrunch that mainly talks about profiles and reviews of the newest internet products and companies.

3. The Gizmodo, the Gadget Guide which by what the title suggests the blog about anything about gadgets like reviews, photos, helpful articles, and anything about what technology has to offer.

4. The Engadget is a blog that is all about the latest and breakthrough gadgets. Articles, breaking news, and other feature stories are provided in this that is all about gadget and its role in technology, entertainment, lifestyle, gaming, finance, and sports.

5. The Boing Boing which is a blog that tackles cultural curiosities and interesting technologies of the world's varying cultures.

6. The Lifehacker, tips and downloads for getting things done blog is all about how to do things in smarter and efficient way.

7. The Ars Technica is also a blog that inform people about the Art of Technology and features like news, analysis, and in-depth coverage of the technology itself.

8. The ReadWriteWeb blog that is responsible in providing Web technology news, reviews and analysis of technological products and the companies that manufactured the products.

9. The Icanhascheezburger blog that offers a wide-ranging information about cats and other animals that include stories, photos, and funny quotes.

10. The Mashable! blog has been recognized as the number one social networking and social media news blog in the world.

The Existence of Blog Hosting Providers

Blog creation was made possible via blog hosting providers. At present, there are thousands and hundreds of blog hosting providers and web hosts that bloggers can choose from.

However, there are certain requirements that should be met so that the blogger can stay in the right environment or rich hosting environment.

Blog hosting represents a flexible web host, a hosting platform that provides features that will make your blog become a big hit.

Some features that you should look for from blog hosting providers:

1. Enough high speed storage
2. Sufficient bandwidth that can actually run a whole blogging empire
3. High disk storage (with at least 1500 GB)
4. Free of charge domain name
5. WebMail addresses
6. MySQL databases
7. Free control panel
8. 24/7 network monitoring
9. Mirrored storage back-ups
10. Unlimited sub-domains
11. Security web hosting services to every blogger Finally, the existence of blog hosting providers paved the way to more and more site listings that are made available to the public. Once you get the service of blog hosts you are able to maximize the things that you are supposed to publish so that you can star maintaining your own blog. So to get started, blog hosts enable you to do the following:

1. Publish blog entries, articles, and other resources for free
2. Image hosting is also free of charge
3. Some blog hosts offer automated news site systems for interactive web sites
4. Blog hosting can also be a kind of publishing service and there are also web hosts that offer such kind of service
5. Blog hosting exclusive for men or women, teenagers and professionals
6. Blog hosting that is intended for education, community, management, and other sectors of the society

In Search of the Right Blog Templates

Finding original skins and templates to personalize your own weblog is a challenge. Though sometimes you can get enough satisfaction from the blog templates provided by blog sites you can always come up with your own and personalized blog template. Get a headstart by familiarizing yourself with the existing blog templates design so that you can come up with something novel.

In fact, there are even blogs that provides wide-ranging blog templates compiled from prevalent blog publishing platform. Apart from the endless features supplied by blogs that offer blog templates there are also a large number of blogs that offer designs from the people who are famous for making blog templates. Powerful designs are introduced and the blogging community or a blogger like you can instantly download your chosen design so you can use it for your benefit.

Indeed, there are more and more blogs that even offer what they call PageKits or website templates that you can use on your weblog. As you download the entire PageKit you also get important features like the HTML and graphics using various formats (.zip format, adobe Photoshop format) for you to completely customize the images using menu options.

Apart from the wide-ranging sources of blog templates, you can also download templates that are easy-to-use and manageable. The web itself is the place of selection if you are looking for the right blog template. Sometimes, you don't even have to come up with your own template because of the widest and a plethora of weblog templates from where you can choose from.

If you are worrying about what background, font, and RSS buttons that you will use for your own blog then the solution is just right in front of your face because there are even blog sites that offer comprehensive and extensive features that will surely get you overwhelmed.

Blog Design Elements: To Create Audience Impact or Not

The blog design elements contribute to the visual factors that in turn tell something about the style of the blogger or the particular author of the blog. However, the contributing factors of the blog design elements do not actually make substantive structural modifications to the layout of the entire blog site. This means, design schemes used by bloggers through weblog software are in fact creating lesser changes of templates.

What are the blog design elements readily available for the bloggers? These are the: screen columns division, use of image, typeface and choice of color, and elements that allow non-textual self-expression or hypertextual features. Hence, if truth be told customized templates are actually the general preference of women while men prefer to unique templates.

Finally, the visual factors that appeal to audience can actually include the following:

1. The colors seen on the blog which can be used in making the words more visible and other texts to be presented.

2. The colors used in the titles and headings.

3. The custom banners which are purposely positioned on the blog site to make it more memorable and attractive. 4. The custom calendar design.

5. The custom cursor along with the cursor movements.
6. The custom fonts.
7. The custom images which are even utilized as their blog design.
8. The custom table borders.
9. The data representations in the forms of counters and quizzes perhaps.
10. The use of more than one language.
11. The use of music that played as the reader navigates the blog.
12. The photographic backgrounds.
13. The text effects like bold, drop shadows, emboss and so on.
14. The use of videos.

Software and Services Used to Create a Blog

At present, people create a blog by using a particular software or service. Every software and service has a defined purpose.

The majority of the software on the Web is actually free of charge. Organizations and groups that offer weblog software also give free server space. The free space is used in housing a specified weblog so that the public can gain free access on it via the Web. Every software contains certain features. So, various commercial versions of the software that provide more features are no longer free. Though, it is also recommended that everybody should start with the basic system of blogging.

However, since the non-commercialized web software is a hit to the public users and web services are even provided for free, they need to employ File Transfer Protocol or FTP so that they can load their weblog to a defined website.

Once a blog is finally created, an instant communication power has also been created. This allows the user to post on their weblog their thoughts and ideas whenever their desire urge them to do so. The great power of the user once again comes in when he or she creates and updates changes to his or her "fairly sophisticated" website.

Though everything seems to sound so sweet and simple, the blogger cannot even claim he is a blogger if he or she doesn't have enough knowledge in web publishing technology at all. In website creation, there are certain documentation and procedures that still need to be done that require knowledge in FTP, website structures, and other technical matters.

If the blogger chooses to deal with more complicated matters, knowledge in creating new templates and HTML is highly a requisite.

Better Search Engine Ranking with a Blog Directory

In general, a directory is any approach done to organize various data or information. The most famous example of a directory is a telephone directory. But there are now other kinds of directories that people turn into when in need to find a list of a certain subject matter like blogs. There are blog directories on the Internet where people can easily search into in order to find the kind of blog site.

Aside from being a helpful list for those who are looking for a certain blog, a blog directory is also helpful for bloggers. People who are into the blogging business and want to rank higher in the search engine usually submit their blog sites to a blog directory. Through this, they can have better ranking in the major search engines and therefore have better readership and more visitors. That will mean better income for those in the blogging business.

When submitting a blog to a blog directory, the blogger is promised of better link building and better income. Among the popular blog directories that many bloggers find useful to submit their blogs to are the Best of the Web Blog Search, Blog Hub, EatonWeb Blog Directory, Bloggernity, and Blogorama. Other names in the list include, the Blog Search Engine, Blog Catalog,

Blog Universe, Globe of Blogs, Blog Universe, Bloggeries, Bigger Blogs, Bloggapedia, and Spillbean. Some bloggers find other blog directories like Blogflux, Blogging Fusion, Bloglisting, Blogio, Blog Explosion, and Super Blog Directory very helpful in link building.

Whatever blog directory the blogger chooses, what's important is that it will create better link building and better optimization on the major search engines. All of the blog directories can do that, but not all can do that effectively.

Why Should Someone Start Blog?

Every blogger has his own reason why he decided to start blog. Blogging is a new craze that replaced the conventional journal making. But bloggers do not just start blog to make his online journal. There are many reasons why people would want to start his own blog. One of the most common reasons to start blog is to have an online journal. Just like the conventional journal, blog can provide for something to release the person's emotional tension.

In fact, according to a certain study, blogging is a great way people use to reduce stress and depression. With blogging, people can express what he feels. But unlike the journal, blogs can also be read by some people like close friends or relatives.

They can help the person in need of emotional support through commenting on his blogs. Other people in similar situation may also read the blog and know that he is not alone in his struggles. Another reason to start a blog is the want to express an opinion. Not everyone can be a good columnist or editor of a publication and express his opinion on a certain matter. But everyone can start blog and be his own editor and columnist. Blogging does not require the good communication skills or a finished degree. It just needs the person's willingness to communicate his opinion with other people. So even a simple citizen can now create a detailed opinion about a specific hot political issue with blogging.

Lastly, some people may also get interested to start blog in order to earn income online. Blogging is not just a good habit now but also a great way to earn extra income online. There are also a lot of ways on how a person can earn through blogging.

People, who love to write about a lot of things and have many different things to say, are generally the ones who are usually told by their Internet-savvy friends to put their writings into good use and place it in blogs.

This, for the simple of reason of having too many words to say, is the reason behind the growing and massive influx of writers towards blogging.

For one, blogs have benefits like relieving stress, and there are writers who write ineligibly, but when asked to write about something, well they deliver.

And writing with a pen on a paper can be very distressing, especially if even the writer himself is unable to read his own handwriting, which clearly does not relieve stress.

Of course the side effect of this lies on the damage on the eyes, but really stress can translate to a whole lot of sickness when left unchecked.

Blogs can also preserve the writings far better than daily bulletin posts at the usual Internet Website like Friendster, and a gift is better shared than kept from others, and the ability to write is a gift considered by many as essential.

For these simple reasons, blogs should be used to benefit many people, and without the blogging sites, there will be no place to best store the writings for future readings and references.

Of course, blogs are still not considered as scholarly readings as these are mostly done through the use of the writers' opinions, but with careful referencing it could be held as one.

On the topic of blogging sites, they are mostly offered for free and rarely does one find a blogging site that is for a price, and there will also be some that will offer financial benefits to those who will write for them.

Yes, blogging is now a job, and for budding writers, this is a shout out.

DROP SHIPPING
What is Dropshipping and How Does It Work?

Dropshipping is a method by which you, as a retailer, sells products to the public without actually holding on to any stock or product. When you sell a product, you send the order directly to your chosen supplier; they ship the product, process the payment, and then send you the difference between the charge they make for the product and the price you charge. You never see the product, you never handle it and you don't need to handle or process any payments. While you don't need to handle the payments, there are some suppliers that will allow you to process your own payments and even some that will allow you to contract your own shipping company. Utilizing these choices, however, defeats the purpose of choosing to run your business using dropshipping.

Some of those differences include the operating margins, operational logistics, operational costs, profit velocity, and barriers to entry.

A Real World Example

Let's assume that you choose to sell guitars. With a traditional store, you would need to buy in physical stock so you buy 25 guitars and store them. Then you would need to find customers who want to purchase the guitars. Let's say that you sell 3 guitars and then sales drop off. You go out of business and end up with a room full of guitars that you can't sell and no money in your bank account. With dropshipping, life is much easier:

- You set up a website with an online store to sell guitars.

- You sell a "Silver Shadow" guitar for $350

- You receive an order for one Silver Shadow through your online store

- That order is sent to your supplier – the manufacturer or wholesaler that you have chosen

- They charge you $200 for the Silver Shadow plus $10 for them to send it directly to your customer

- The supplier will pack the order and ship the Silver Shadow to your customer

- You make $90 on the sale

- Repeat as much as you can and watch the profits grow.

In some cases, the payments will be processed by the supplier and they will send you the difference between your price and theirs, less any shipping costs.

While there are many advantages to choosing to build and run a traditional ecommerce business instead of creating a business that uses dropshipping, there are significantly less risks associated with using dropshipping.

Understanding Dropshipping

Comparing the method of dropshipping to the tradition ecommerce store has already shown some of the pros and cons to using dropshipping for your business. Below we are going to analyze the pros and cons as they apply specifically to a business using dropshipping.

Dropshipping does have a number of pros and cons to it and you need to understand these before you attempt to get involved in the business. Understanding the following pros and cons will help you to ensure you are making the best choice for you and your business and will also make sure you aren't surprised by any of the things you encounter as you set up and begin running your business.

Pros

Less Capital

This is, without a doubt, the single biggest advantage to dropshipping. Anyone can launch their own ecommerce store without the need to have vast amounts of capital to invest thousands of dollars upfront in stock. Traditional retailing requires a person to have money tied up in inventory – dropshipping eliminates that hurdle.

With dropshipping, there is no need to make any purchases until the sale is made and the money is paid by the customer. This allows you to start your own ecommerce business today with little money in hand. In fact, there are even some platforms you can use to set up your ecommerce business absolutely free of charge. Although these options aren't usually as successful as other platforms, it is a way to make a little bit of money to put towards creating a better business model.

Easy to Get Going

Running your own ecommerce business has never been easier, especially as you no longer need to handle physical products. When you choose dropshipping, you no longer need to consider:

- Renting or managing warehouse space
- Packing orders and shipping them
- Tracking your inventory for accounting
- Handling returned items
- Handling inbound shipments
- Having to order products and managing your inventory levels

The Blueprint

The process of setting up your online store doesn't need to be a complicated one. In fact, if you know the steps to follow, and are aware of some do's and don'ts, you can do it in a relatively short period of time without becoming overwhelmed or confused. This chapter is going to outline exactly what information you need to know before you dive into the world on running an online business that uses suppliers that dropship their products to your customers.

Selecting Your Product

Before you can even begin setting up your store, you need to know what product you are going sell in your store.

Look For Product Ideas

Without a product to sell, there is no reason to open a business. Before you begin searching for new ideas on what you should sell, start with what you already have, or how can you solve your own problems or the problems of the people you know. Some questions to ask yourself are:

- What products or niches are you interested in?

- What products are your friends passionate about?

- What issues are you having in your own life? What products would solve it?

- What sort of businesses are around your community? Can they be turned into an online concept? What businesses in your community would appeal to people outside your community?

- What products are trending in other parts of the world? Is there a demand for them in your community? Can you create a demand for them in your community?

- If you are unsure about products, is there a particular industry you want to be involved in? What products are popular in that industry? What products from that industry would you find useful?

- What products are popular in other online stores? Is there a specialty to this product you can specialize in selling?

- What's trending on social curations sites? Is there an untapped product out there that people would love to see made available to them?

Understanding Your Market

Perhaps the most important thing to consider is your target audience (to whom you will sell your product). You aren't going to be able to run a successful business if you are selling wedding supplies and dog toys together on the same site. The same is true if you are selling cheap t-shirts next to designer clothes.

There are thousands of products and services available to consumers. This means that there are unlimited ways you can enter the marketplace. Before you can dive right in, you need to figure out who your target customers. Knowing who you are selling to will ensure you are choosing the right product for those people. Below are some tips on how to define your target market.

Remember, you can have different target markets that might fit into different niches of the product you are looking to sell. Consider the following point for each target market separately.

Choose Specific Demographics

- Age – This can be the age of the purchaser, and the age of the user if they are different.

- Gender – Like age, this can be the gender of the purchaser and user.

- Location

- Income Level

- Education Level

- Marital Status

- Occupation

- Ethnic Background

Consider The Psychographics

- Values

- Personality

- Attitudes

- Interests

- Lifestyles

- Behavior

Evaluate Your Decision

- Is there a large enough population of people who meet your criteria?

- Are they easily reached with your message?

- Will your target market see a need for your product?

- Do you understand what drives your target market to make decisions?

- Can your target market afford your product?

- Will the target market benefit from your product?

Some Other Tips When Choosing A Product:

- Know your competition

- Is the product something you are knowledgeable about if you aren't knowledgeable about the product you are going to be selling, ensure that you become knowledgeable before you dive into running the business. Knowing the ins and outs of the products will ensure that you are able to provide effective customer service.

Choosing the supplier

The supplier you work with is one of the biggest decisions you are going to have to make when you start up your online store. The supplier you partner with has a large impact on the success of your business, and you want to make sure you choose the right one.

Before you begin searching for your supplier, there are a couple of things you need to do:

1. Make sure you can prove you are a retailer. Have your business' EIN number as well as a copy of your resale certificate.

2. Be familiar with dropshipping terminology as well as the common practices of dropshipping before you contact any potential suppliers.

Once you are familiar with dropshipping, you are ready to set out and find your supplier.

Know Your Industry

Different industries have different supply chains. If you are running a small boutique with a specific, specialized item you are going to be more successful if you partner with a manufacturer or a small local supplier. If you are going to run a larger store with many products, you are going to be looking for a supplier with a larger selection of products they are selling.

Don't Rely On Search Engines To Find Suppliers

Most suppliers do not prioritize search engine optimization. This means you aren't going to be able to find them by running a search through Google.

- Use Trade Magazines – If you can find magazines or newsletters that are geared towards your particular industry, you are going to find suppliers looking for you. Many of these publications also have websites with past issues which can offer your more resources.

- Forums And Online Groups – If you can find a forum or online group that is specific to dropshipping or your industry, you may be able to find out what suppliers other members are using.

- Trade Shows Or Conferences – If you are able to attend a trade show or conference, you may be able to directly interact with potential suppliers.

Other Options

Curated Lists: Curated lists are available, if you pay to access them. However, some of the entries can be outdated or obsolete.

Using Google: This can be incredibly time consuming as many suppliers aren't concerned with their online presence. If you are going to use Google to search, skip ahead to page ten or so and begin your search there.

Setting Up The Webstore

Before you begin setting up your webstore, you should have the business aspects already figured out. This includes your company name, the products you are going to be selling, and the prices for your products. The next things you are going to need are:

- A domain name and extension
- A web host
- A dedicated IP address
- A private SSL certificate
- A shopping cart script
- A payment gateway

Once you have the above things, you are ready to set up your website. You have two choices when it comes to setting you your website. You can either create a home page and other static pages (e.g., product background) or you can use your shopping cart script as a standalone for your entire website.

Building A Website

If you are choosing to build a website entirely, without using the shopping cart script, it is likely going to take more time and work. It is also going to require you to have working knowledge of HTML, styling, and CSS. Assuming you have knowledge on these things the next steps are:

-Design: You need to have a basic idea of how you want your site to be designed before you start out. One of the first things to know is that your font choices are limited. Next you are going to need to know which images are going to be displayed as images and which are going to be backgrounds for one of your pages.

-Preparation: You are going to need to know the measurements for your design. This includes the width and height of columns, spacing between them as well as the total of everything combined. Essentially you are going to need the dimensions of every major element on the site. You will need the minor ones too, but not until later in the set up. Next, you are going to need to develop your site using HTML and CSS.

Deployment: Once your website is designed and set up, you need to deploy it. This typically doesn't involve more than uploading it to your web server.

If you decide to use the shopping cart script as a standalone for your site, you will use the steps outlined here:

Installation: First you are going to need to install the shopping cart system. You can auto install the system if you look under the software/services section in your hosting page. There may be some minor changes depending on the host and system you choose to use, but it will be similar.

When you install the system, you will also set an installation folder. This will dictate where users are going to go when they enter your store (such as directly to the product page, or an about page etc.)

-Customization: The first thing you should do is change the logo and remove the footer graphic.

Setting Up The Ecommerce

A shopping cart system of some sort is essential if you are going to be processing payments through your site. Once you have set up a shopping cart system these are the next steps:

- Obtain an internet merchant account from your bank- This will enable you to accept credit card payments online
- Obtain a payment gateway account- This is an online processor which exchanges information from your customer's credit card to your internet merchant account and authorizes the credit card information

Things To Keep In Mind While Conducting Business

There are a few important things you are going to want to keep in mind as you embark on the journey of opening an online business using the dropshipping model.

- Customer Satisfaction – Your customer is a person, even if you never see or speak to them. Put yourself in your customer's shoes, you want your customer to be happy and this is best done with good customer service.

- Keep An Active Mailing List. – Offer a reward, such as free shipping, for signing up and you can use their email address to send out newsletters about new product offerings and sales to keep your customers coming back.

- Don't Oversell – No one wants to feel pressured into buying something. Pointing out the advantages to a product is great, but you don't want to lose customers because you are pointing out the features of a product too frequently.

- Keep Customers Coming Back – Repeat visitors are a great way to increase your sales. Writing helpful articles about the products you are selling, hosting sales, and unique content will keep your customers coming back.

- Respond Quickly – When visitors to your site send you emails or fill out their information for your mailing list, it is important to respond as quickly as possible. People will remember how long it took you to respond to them and often appreciate a quick turnaround in response to an email.

Getting Your Own Dropshipping Business Off the Ground

Starting your own dropshipping business is easier than you think and it comes with some fantastic advantages – not having to answer to anyone but yourself, reaping the rewards for the effort you put in and the flexibility to choose from where you work. Unfortunately, most people think one or more of these three thing when they consider starting up their own business online:

- I don't have the time to run a business

- I don't have the money needed to run this business

- I don't have any of the skills needed to run an online business

These are nothing more than excuses. You don't need a lot of time – in fact, the most time you spend will be in setting up your online store. Once you know how to do it, you can start up and full functioning ecommerce store in less than a day.

You don't need vast amounts of money because you are not buying any stock or having to pay expensive overhead. All you need money for is the startup – the website, hosting domain name etc. and, if you shop around, you can get some great deals on these.

In terms of skill, well you do need a little but it isn't difficult to come by. Most hosting companies offer package deal that include a domain name and a website builder, complete with full instructions on how to do it. You do not need to be a computer programmer or coder anymore and, if you choose products that you can build a blog around, you can even get the website for free by using WordPress.

To begin your new business, you need one thing:

A webstore

You can't sell products online without having a webstore – this is the functioning part of the entire process of dropshipping. The webstore is the part that your customers see, where they order their products from; they don't see what goes on behind the scenes and they don't care very much either. A webstore should be easy for your customers to navigate and should also be visually friendly and welcoming. In times gone by, the only way to build a website was to be proficient at coding. While you can still build a website using coding to make it completely your own there are definitely other options. These days, the process is all but automatic and these are the steps you need to follow to set up a WordPress website (WordPress is one of the easiest to get started with):

Get your domain name and a hosting package set up.

A domain name is how potential visitors find you and your site that you have worked so hard on. Since the internet is based on IP addresses and not domain names, every web server requires a Domain Name System to translate the domain name to the IP address. A good domain name makes you much more accessible to your clients. For example, in the URL www.WordPress.com, the domain name is "WordPress.com." "WordPress" is the main part of the domain name and the ".com" is the extension.

Some extensions include: .com for businesses, . org for organizations, .mobi for sites that are only for mobile devices, .net is used for both business and organizations and .me is used for personal projects.

For a business, the best extension to use is .com. This is one of the most popular extensions and for this reason, it is also more expensive to register. However, if your business is recommended by word of mouth, it is most often what people are going to type in if they only know your company name. A way around this is to use a cheaper variant like .net and have your domain name flow with it in such a way it becomes part of your company name, for example, shopforyourpet.net. The rhyme and flow will allow for your extension to be part of the name when your customers are telling friends about your products.

Sometimes it is a good idea to register your business with more than one extension. For example, if your site is awesomeshirts.com, you might consider also registering awesomeshirts.net and awesomeshirts.info so the competition can't ride on your coattails by using the same domain name and a different extension. Since a domain name isn't expensive, it never hurts to play it safe, especially as your business grows. If you do this, you can purchase and park the domain. This means that the domain is yours, but there is no content on it which protects it from being used by anyone else. It is also a good idea to do this if the domain you choose has a popularly misspelled word in it.

Once you have your domain name, you need to choose a good webhost. The domain name is nothing more than a signpost, which directs users to the server that is holding your website. This server must be capable of running what is needed for your website, in the way that you need it to be run. This is the most expensive bit of starting your own dropshipping business but you don't need to spend a fortune – look around and you will find some good deals but use these criteria to do so:

● Check user reviews but look on review sites that are independent to the host you are considering

● Make sure the host is able to run WordPress

● Check that the host runs cPanel, DirectAdmin or some other similar system as their back end. What this means is that you will be able to install WordPress with just a single click.

● Check out their customer service – user reviews will tell you what you need to know as well

● Make sure they have fast servers in the country or countries that your webstore is targeting.

Then proceed to the following steps:

Install WordPress

WordPress is the easiest of all the platforms to build a website on, removing all of the coding out and leaving you to concentrate on the content of your website. WordPress a common site that is used by a wide variety of people such as bloggers, news outlets, Fortune 500 companies and even celebrities. WordPress is free and can be used to run just about any type of site from a forum to a directory, as well as a coupon site, a job board, a booking system, a support desk, a place for classified ads, and of course, an online store. By choosing to use WordPress as a framework, you will be able to build your own application on top of its existing APIs and built in functionality regarding user management and security. This will allow you to create a site that is unique and easy to set up and also easily used by your customers. As I mentioned before, your host should run cPanel or DirectAdmin – cPanel is the most common and easiest to use. Part of the reason cPanel is more common is that it splits its features into categories which makes it easier to find specific features. CPanel also provides more features and plugins than DirectAdmin, which gives more choices to how you are going to set up your site. When you sign up for your host, you will receive an email giving you full instructions on how to install WordPress – for DirectAdmin, you need to click on the link that says "Installatron Applications Installer", while in cPanel, the link will say, "Install WordPress in 1 Click".

Click on these and follow the on-screen instructions for WordPress to be easily installed.

Installing and Configuring WordPress Themes

One of the best parts about WordPress is that you can customize what is actually a very basic framework to fit your needs. To make your website look good and appeal to potential customers you need to choose a theme and install it. A theme is nothing more than a template that is pasted over the top of WordPress and you can find a vast array of different ones – some free, some not.

While there are thousands of options for themes, you don't want just to click on the first one you see that you like and assume it is going to work for your business. There are a couple things you should consider before making a final choice on the theme you are going to use.

- Simplicity – You probably aren't going to want a theme that comes with lots of colors, complex layouts, and flashy animations. While these would be effective for some sites, a site that is trying to sell, products should be kept simple and neat and allow the products to be the star of the site, not the background.

- Responsiveness – A responsive theme is one that adjusts its layout to different screen sizes and devices. Since a lot of web traffic is generated from mobile and other handheld devices, a theme that is going to respond accordingly is a huge advantage and will make navigation easier for your customers. If your theme is not responsive, you may lose customers to other web stores that do provide responsiveness.

The theme you select should also relate to the product you are going to sell, or at least not be contradictive. For example, don't use a beach theme if you are going to sell snowshoes, whereas a theme that is all in blues or greens would be appropriate for selling any products.

Choose your theme and then you can go ahead and tweak it to your personal needs. These are the main things you will want to change to make your theme truly personal to you:

● The logo – change it to your own

● General settings – This is where you will paste in the tracking code you will be given if you choose to use Google Analytics

● Side panels and sliders – if your theme has these you will want to configure them to have some content in them

● Subscribe and Connect module – this is where your customers will subscribe to your email list and to your social media profiles.

Your theme is now configured to look amazing and tempt potential customers to both explore the site and the products you are advertising.

Install an ecommerce Plugin

WordPress does not include webstore functionality but it does allow plugins. Choose a good ecommerce plugin – one of the best and easiest is WooCommerce but you do need a compatible theme – and install it and activate it.

You will need to configure your plugin with basic information, like currency, shipping costs, etc. Configure anything that needs to be changed but do pay attention specifically to the following:

● *Pages*

The pages on your webstore are important for guiding your customers to the information they are looking for. There are eight pages that you are going to want to make sure your webstore has to promote optimal customer navigation.

- Welcome: The welcome page is used to welcome customers to your store and share any important or useful information that you feel the customer should get as an introduction.

- About Us: The about us page is used to give potential customers the information they want to know to convince them to choose to shop with you instead of someone else. This page should be personable detailed. It isn't enough to say you are the best at what you are offering; you should prove it.

- Contact Us: The contact us page is used to give customers options on how they can contact you to give you feedback or ask questions. This page can include a contact form that can be filled out as well as an email address if they prefer to email from their email account instead of filling out the form. If you have a phone number, it is also useful to include it and the hours you can be reached at on this page.

- New Product: A new product page will allow your customers see the new products you are offering to encourage repeat business. Customers may come to your site just to see what new products you are offering.

- Top Products: Customers purchase the top products most often. You want to put products on this page that are the ones most likely to appeal to new customers and have high reviews which will encourage customers to come back and shop more.

- Promotions: Used to let your customers know of any promotions you are running.

- Privacy Policy: This is a legal notice that tells your customers how you are using the personal information they provide to your business.

- Terms and Conditions: This is used to govern the relationship between your customers and you; it is a legal contract. It will cover payment terms, shipping terms, and any other important information.

You can also choose to add any additional custom pages you feel fit with your webstore and increase customer usability such as information pages or news items that might pertain to your products.

Ensure that all of your pages are configured correctly – if any are missed, or if they won't work properly.

- ***Taxes***

This will depend on your country of origin but most require you to make it very clear which, if any taxes are being applied. Make sure that he plugin is configured to show the taxes at checkout.

- *Payment Settings*

It's fantastic when you start getting customers but it's all meaningless if you don't give them a way to pay – this only applies in cases where you will be taking the payment for your dropshipped products. Where the supplier processes the payment, this is not necessary.

- *Shipping*

You need to let your customers know how much they can expect to pay for shipping. Even if you do not pass these costs on to your customers, you still need to configure the settings properly to ensure the customer is not being charged more or less than they should be. This also allows the customers to be aware of the charges they can expect when they complete the purchase.

Populate Your Products

By now, you should have a domain name, a hosting package and a fully functioning WordPress website. Now it's time to add in some products to sell. The next logical step is to choose your suppliers and I will get to that later. For the purposes of this, you just need to know how to add them.

Make sure that your product title is clear, not too long, and is easy to understand. It must contain some details about your product. Next, you must make sure that your product description is clear, detailed and easy to understand. Make sure your product categories are clearly labelled, as are the product type, shipping type, price, article code and any other information the customer needs to see. Dividing your products into categories is an important way to prevent overwhelming your customers. You want to ensure each category page is simple, well organized and doesn't overwhelm your customers. If a product falls into more than one category, it can be posted more than once so the customer can find it easily regardless of where they look.

Adding images is also vital – most people will not buy without seeing what the product looks like. You can use the image that your chosen suppliers use. Ensure you don't use too many pictures, as people tend to skim and don't appreciate the visual variety if there are too many to look at. However, it is important to ensure a complete product description, as customers are more likely to remember a product that has been verbally described to them. Ensure you tell the customer how he can use your products and why it's the one he should want to buy.

Now you have chosen and registered a domain name and extension that is going to effectively guide customers to your webstore. You have been able to successfully set up your store with a theme that is simple and inviting, and the pages are laid out in a way that is user friendly and allows your customers to navigate to what they are looking for without getting frustrated.

That really is all it takes to set up a good ecommerce storefront for selling your dropship products. In the next chapter, we will look at how to choose the right products.

Choosing the Right Products

The biggest hurdle you will have to overcome is in choosing the right niche and the right products to focus your attention on. This decision is crucial to whether your dropshipping business succeeds or fails. The single biggest mistake you will make is to choose a product that is based on your own passions or personal interests, especially if you want to build up a truly successful dropshipping business – you have to supply what other people want, not what you want. Especially if you aren't the type of person to follow trends or are the type of person who is often considered to be "outside the box."

How to choose the right product

Market research can seem overwhelming, but it is essential to ensuring your product is going to appeal to the people you are going to be reaching with your site. If you already have an idea of what you want to sell, you can check the market trends to see how that product is currently doing on the market. If you aren't sure what you want to sell, market trends can still be useful to you. Market trends are able to give you an idea of what products people are currently buying, or have interest in buying.

It can also be a great idea to choose a product that isn't easily obtainable locally or a local product that is coveted by an area outside where it is currently available. Another suggestion is to find a product based on the interests of your target audience. This can be in the form of a new TV show or fashion trend that is starting.

This also extends to looking for an opportunity gap. If you are choosing a product that is already being sold by many different competitors, find something you can do different or better than everyone else. This can be an improved product feature, a market completely missed by your competitors or even something in your marketing strategy.

If you are going to sell a product based on something that is currently trending, ensure you are capitalizing on the trend early. At the beginning of a trend, there tend to be more people who are purchasing the product. If you get onto the bandwagon at the end of the trend, everyone else is already moving on to the next thing. Unless you think you are going to revive a dying trend, don't wait too long to capitalize on a trend in the market.

It is important to take the product turnover into consideration when you are making your choices. A product line that changes year to year is going to require a lot more time and energy to ensure that your product list is kept up-to-date and doesn't contain last year's options, which may no longer be available. A product with a lower turnover will allow you to invest in a more informative website that is going to be applicable for a longer period of time.

While there may be fewer potential customers, there is also going to be less competition which will result in it being easier to get to the top of search engines and can be much more cost effective in terms of advertising. The right product is an instrumental component to your success, take your time and don't rush into the first product that looks good.

To build up a successful business you must be able to do one of the following:

Have Access to Exclusive Distribution or Pricing

Being able to arrange exclusive agreements for products or exclusive pricing will give you the edge to selling online without the need to buy in or make your own product. These are not easy things to arrange and you may find that you are still outpriced because other dropshippers will still sell the same or similar at wholesale prices.

If you can get exclusive distribution you need to find a way to convince your customers that the product you are selling is of better quality than the competition, especially if the competition is offering a knock off product at a lower price.

Sell at the Lowest Possible Price

Low price is not always the main driving force behind a customer's decision to buy. Customers tend to want to spend their money on a product with the highest value and the lowest risk. This means that you need to convince them that spending a little more money on your product is the better choice because there is less risk and more value to them.

Add Your Value Outside of the Price

Think in terms of providing information that complements your chosen products. A true entrepreneur will solve problems, selling products at premium prices at the same time. Make sure you an offer guidance and knowledgeable advice within your specific niche. One highly effective way to add value to your products outside the price is through your customer service. If you are able to answer all your customer's questions without them having to contact you, and are able to respond quickly to any emails, it is going to make your web store stand out above the others.

Adding Value

This isn't always easy and this will work better for some niches than it will others. Look for key characteristics that will make it easy to add value with content, especially in niches that:

Have Several Components

If a product is made up of several different components, potential customers are more likely to look for information on the internet. For example, if you buy a new chair for your office, it's a simple purchase. If, on the other hand you were to buy a complete home surveillance security system, you would want to know how each part of the system works and how it all works together.

The more components and the more variety that can be offered in these components, the better the opportunity to build up your value by offering information and education on the products.

If the product you are offering falls into this category, and is also not a product line that changes every year, you have a great opportunity to build up an informative site that will help your customers understand why they should buy from you. It will also help them build trust with you since you will be providing answers to all of their questions about the product without them having to spend their time talking to someone over the phone or going into a store to speak to someone.

Are Confusing or Customizable

This goes on the same vein as above – if a product is customizable or the choice is confusing, your value come in being able to offer guidance and education on what to use where, how to use a specific product and how to customize it.

Again, if this product is from a line that isn't constantly changing, you can easily create an informative site. If the customizations are constantly changing, it may make it more difficult to build up an information hub, but depending on the product it is by no means impossible, especially if the main component of the product remains the same, since it's the information on the main component that is going to be more important than the customizations.

Require Installation or Setup

This is perhaps one of the easiest to choose – products that need to be installed or set up technically, especially if they are not easy ones. Go back to the home security system – let's say that you were choosing one and one website offered a system with a 2 page set up document and the other offered a detailed guide that ran to several pages, including troubleshooting. Which one would you buy? Offering up the most information and guidance is the best way to gain customers.

How to Add value

Adding value to your product is fairly simple and can be accomplished in several ways:

- Creating detailed buyer guides
- Creating detailed listings and product descriptions
- Creating installation guides and setup information
- Creating detailed videos showing how a particular product works
- Creating a guide or system for product compatibility

Picking the Best Customers

Even once you have established your target market or customer pool, it is important to know that there are many different demographic types within it. You want to be aware of what demographic is going to be interested in your product and how to best appeal to the demographic you want to target.

You can't lump all customers under the same umbrella – you might find that a customer who buys a small, cheaper priced item will expect you to go to the moon and back for them while a customer who purchases something more expensive will probably ask for nothing more from you than the item they are purchasing.

There are a few other considerations you must take into account when you are choosing a product to sell:

- **Price**

You must consider your price point in relation to how the pre-sales service you provide to your customers. Most people will happily place an order online for $200 without the need to talk to someone on the phone first, however, if you are selling an item that costs $1,000, your customers might not be so eager. Most will want to talk to someone about the product first, and not to just about the item but also to make sure they are dealing with a genuine store.

- **MAP Pricing**

There are manufacturers who set a MAP (minimum advertised price) for their particular products and they will require all sellers to sell at or above a certain level. This stops price wars, which is a common problem with dropshipping, and also means that you can realize a good profit margin.

Look for manufacturers that enforce MAP pricing and your business will gain profits immensely. With all competitors selling at the same price, it will all come down to how strong and convincing your website and sales pitch is and you won't need to worry about being knocked out of the market by cheaper prices.

- **Marketing Potential**

The marketing potential of your business is the entire size of the market for your product. You want to make sure you are going to be able to get the word out about your web store to as many people within the market as possible and to do this you need to have an effective plan. A good plan will include advertising, often through free platforms.

The day you launch your new business is too late for thinking about marketing – this has to be thought about well in advance. Website promotion is the only way you will bring in new customers so set up social media pages, write articles, set up a blog and get involved in forums that are in your niche.

- **Plenty of Accessories**

Accessories are something that can be added to your product to make it more versatile, useful, or attractive. It can also be used to personalize a common product and make it more individual. If the product you choose to sell comes along with the option of accessories, it is a good idea to include as many of them as possible in your web store. Customers like to be able to make their products their own and express their individuality.

As a general retail rule of thumb, the margins on high priced items are lower than those on the lower-priced accessories that go with it. Take the humble smartphone for example; most people will shop around for the best price but when it comes to the case that goes with it, they are less likely to do that. Instead, they will buy it from the place they buy their phone. Being able to offer compatible accessories for big-ticket items will bring customers flocking in. This is especially true when you are able to find accessories that most other retailers aren't offering. This is a situation when using more than one supplier for your web store can prove to be exceptionally beneficial.

- **Low Turnover**

By now, you should now that, if you can provide information, guides, and education with your products, you are more likely to make a sale. Yet, if your chosen product is of a type that changes every year, like the smartphone, the work involved in keeping your site maintained is going to be huge. Stick to products that don't get updated on a regular basis and keep your website going for much longer.

- **Hard to Find**

Don't be too specific here –if you can sell a product that can't be found too easily locally, you stand a better chance of reaping the rewards. If a person wanted to buy a new hoe or garden fork, they would just go down to their nearest hardware store. However, selling something a bit more specific, like falcon training equipment, for example, will bring in a certain number of customers.

- ### Small is the New Large

Most people expect free shipping these days but if you opt to sell large expensive items, you will either lose money when you have to pay the shipping or you will lose customers because they won't pay the shipping. Keeping your products small will make it easier for you to ship out free or cheap.

Picking the right niche is not easy and you need to take lots of different thing into consideration first. These are the main guidelines that you need to think about when you come to picking your product

When it comes to choosing the product you want to sell in your web store, the options are endless and it can be overwhelming to begin narrowing down the options in order to find the product that is going to give you the optimal sales and profit. By putting some thought and research into the product you want to sell, you are going to ensure that you are choosing a product that is going to appeal to the customers who are in the target market you are striving to reach. Knowing the potential competition of a product will tell you if there is room in the market for you and how you can squeeze yourself in effectively.

Finding a valuable product will take some time and work. It will also take some work to find the accessories and add-ons that will best complement it. However, once you find these things, you are going to be able to put together an interesting ecommerce site and begin to turn a profit.

Once you have found your spot in the market and made a final decision on your product, the next thing you are going to have to do is find a supplier that you can rely on to have the product you need in stock and ship it out to your customers in a timely manner.

E-COMMERCE
The future of marketing

The online space has become a different world than it used to be. It used to be very simple to sell things online, but since we've moved into a more conscious usage of the Internet, people are more concerned about their security and their personal information being stolen. This explains the reluctance to input credit card information.

And that is exactly why we must optimize our websites to continuously understand what is working and what is not. If you don't optimize, measure, and iterate, you're probably not growing your business as fast as you possibly can. You're losing out on a lot of opportunities and wasting a lot of money in the process.

But what if you had an optimization plan? You have a sound process, a system you follow that helps you grow your business and take it to the next level. An optimization plan can help you spend the right amount of time, resources, and effort to test and make sound decisions to increase profit. This book will give you that plan.

I was recently quoted on Forbes.com as saying, "Every year we advance toward data-driven marketing. All design, advertising, and social media will be focused on driving measurable results using cutting-edge tracking and predictive analytics. Websites will focus more on optimizing conversion rates and increasing website traffic because it doesn't matter how much traffic you drive to your website if you're not converting that traffic into actual sales."

Small Business, Big Money Online is entirely focused on helping you make better decisions. You will be able to utilize the tools I recommend for your marketing and conversion rate optimization to get real, proven results — increasing conversions, generating more leads, and maximizing your return on investment.

Customer mindset

To optimize successfully and efficiently, you must adopt the right mindset. The mindset you need is one of growth, not only from the perspective of being abundant and forward thinking, but also about your business as a whole.

During my years as a web designer, I never took a single marketing or business class. I learned everything through personal, hands-on experience and trial and error. And it was a *lot* easier to sell online from 2000 to 2006. We used to be able to simply put up a landing page and get a ton of leads and a very high conversion rate.

But today, it's a different story. We need to understand our business holistically, and we need to know our ideal customers. The right mindset will help you realize that consumers no longer buy the way they used to. We need to study the different types of personas coming to the website and know where they're going—consequently leading them through the ideal click M.A.P. This stands for the Marketing Along Path. This is the streamlined path you want the visitor to follow to become a customer.

You must execute goal-oriented strategies instead of relying on random marketing efforts. Come up with your own system—or use one that's already been created. This book will show you my system, and as you read through, you'll start to see a pattern of opportunity.

Buyer legends

Buyer Legends is a process detailed in a book written by Bryan and Jeffrey Eisenberg. It is based on their signature framework Persuasion Architecture™, which you will learn about later. It becomes important as a blueprint to help us outline our customers' journey through our websites. We need to understand how people interact with our site and how they feel about our brands. Buyer Legends helps you deliver on the promise of your brand. This concept—creating narrative or story—is increasingly finding its way into the marketing world. The story that matters most is the story that takes place between the company and the customer. Without a story, all that's there is just data, more or less static. If you do not understand the context—the story of the interaction between the customer and the brand—you can interpret nothing.

But until now, the tools you've been given to understand the customers' actions have either been focused solely on the brand through the brand's story and branding or on the customer through personas. The tools have not focused on the decision-based marketing, shopping, buying, and experience that happens in the linked brand-and-customer experience. To understand this dynamic, you need to create the story. And this is where Buyer Legends comes in. Buyer Legends is a simple scenario narrative that helps identify the gap between the brand story and the brand experience. Buyer Legends ensures that all business decisions are made directly by the team responsible for the results and not indirectly through the creative, retail, customer service, legal, technology, or sales teams. Using Buyer Legends is fundamentally different. It's hard work to think something completely through before doing it. There is a tremendous urge for us to take immediate action and start production, and this goes against that. You want to outline the story before you start creating any marketing material. That is how you begin to build the different personas for your ideal customers.

Once we have an understanding of the story from the buyers' points of view, we can then establish the ideal click M.A.P. for the customer. You want to map out your customer along a specific path. This is where we define our M.A.P. (Market Along Path). Ideally, you want to understand which pages each of your customer personas land on and create a M.A.P.for each of those different marketing experiences and campaigns. This is how you can get customers to convert with much less effort.

Ideal click M.A.P.

To have successful marketing campaigns, you need to learn from experience. You'll need to use the insight you've gained over the years of running your business. As you gain this intellect and intuition, it will become your mindset. Your mind will shift from thinking that you need to drive more traffic or spend more money on advertising to realizing that you should instead be trying to increase the number of people who spend money with you. Instead of driving traffic, we are now going to focus on improving conversions. We need to ask ourselves, *what happens post click?* After potential clients or customers arrive at your website, how can you lead them through a specific and ideal click map that will get them from start to finish?

M.A.P. stands for marketing along a specific path. Creating your ideal M.A.P. will lead your target audiences through a specific set of pages, defining their journey. Here's a definitive example of a M.A.P. for eCommerce. An individual types a keyword into Google then clicks on a pay-per-click advertising campaign. This then leads them to a landing page. The landing page could be a custom web page, a category page, a specific product detail page, or even your homepage. I don't recommend sending paid advertising to your homepage, however. The landing page should have one focus that directly helps the visitor with the problem (query) they were searching for in Google. The solution to that problem is the goal for that instance of the M.A.P. That conversion goal could be a lead, a sale, or just a click.

In eCommerce, when a customer lands on a product category page, they are more likely to click an item, and from that item, they will be directed to a product detail page. This is the page where they can add something to a cart. Once they click "add to cart", they are then sent to a shopping cart page where they can view items in their shopping cart basket and then click to check out. As they go through the checkout process, they're eventually taken to a thank you or confirmation page.

This is the ideal M.A.P. for an eCommerce. You want to create a M.A.P. specific to your particular marketing experience while keeping the customer's best interests a priority.

Persuasion architecture

You need to think of your customer as the center of the universe. For each type of customer, you want to understand the different types of personas that visit your websites. A persona is a particular type of individual who is visiting your websites. It is more than just average demographics—personas also take into account the overall goal of the individual, how they use your websites, and the customer's voice.

Persuasion Architecture™ is the framework that Bryan Eisenberg and his brother Jeffrey created to persuade customers when they ignore marketing. Persuasion Architecture™ begins with the premise that the buying decision process and the sales process must work in tandem. The solution for dramatically improving conversion rates does not lie in helping businesses "sell better." It lies in helping businesses marry the sales process to their audience's buying decision processes—in essence, the business must provide a structure that helps the prospect "buy better."

For you to achieve your goals, your visitors must first achieve their goals. Only when you help your audience buy better will you be able to sell better.

The Phases of Persuasion Architecture™:

Persuasion Architecture has six phases. The process begins with Uncovery, continues with Wireframing, Storyboarding, and Prototyping, and then enters the actual coding phase in Development. The final phase provides for testing, measuring, and optimization, an ongoing process that ensures your management decisions are always based on solid information. The following pages describe each phase of Persuasion Architecture in more depth.

- **Uncovery**
  Uncovering the buyer personas through narratives
- **Wireframing**
  Wireframing out every single step and persona along the entire journey
- **Storyboarding**
  Storyboarding the creative
- **Protoyping**
  Prototyping the design and functionality
- **Development**
  Developing the final experience
- **Optimizing**
  Optimization and testing measurement

Uncovery

The goals of Uncovery are to match the value of your business to what matters most to the customer. To better understand the customer, you'll start to create customer "personas," which are almost like narrative avatars of your customers. You will develop stories of your customers as they are walking through their buying process and encountering your business. What do they see? What key words or phrases in your value proposition attract them? How do their needs, wants and desires fit with your business objectives? Uncovery, the first step toward designing and developing effective persuasion architecture, follows a logical four-step process:

Step 1. Analyze your business, from your business model and products to customers and competitors.

Step 2. Identify your business goals and objectives and your key performance indicators.

Step 3. Develop your customer personas.

Step 4. Develop the scenarios for those personas.

Wireframing

Wireframing is a detailed "mapping" of your sales process for the personas' buying process. In other words, you "follow" them as they navigate through your website, taking into account any possible path that they might take. Through the links in your wireframe, you will see the site from the perspective of the customer, and this will generate useful feedback at a time when changes are easy.

Storyboarding

This phase of Persuasion Architecture focuses on persuasive content, layout and design. If the wireframe is the "what" of Persuasion Architecture, the storyboard is the "how." The goal here is to flesh out the wireframe, filling in the words and the graphics.
Start with the persuasive copy: everything that has to be written. You already had some barebones text in the wireframe. Now focus on making that text persuasive.
Next, you create a first mockup of the storyboard. You'll be considering different elements, ranging from branding and navigation to detailed issues such as header graphics and even copyrights and privacy notices.
The next step is to move toward the actual design of the site. Start in grayscale: you want to see how the structure and words work with the emotional impact of color. Once you have your full design in grayscale, add the color. A color scheme is important for a variety of reasons, including the emotional feel of your site and cohesiveness of the different pages.

The final step is your image into an HTML document, with the usual web considerations (e.g., choosing fonts that can be read easily, using cascading sheets for simplicity, and so on).

Prototyping:

The next phase of Persuasion Architecture is to create a prototype, just as architects create full models of their final buildings. Your prototype will be an actual operational model of your site. Make all the changes you can think of now — it's still easy and cheap.

Development:

This final phase should be the easiest because all of the decisions have been made in the previous phases. The only function now is to program — or more accurately, have your developers create the programming — to transform what you've planned and decided into reality.

Optimization:

You now have a finished product, and it's time for the final phase testing and measuring. You will now learn through monitoring your Web analytics whether your decisions in the previous phases meet your expectations and objectives. And if they don't, you'll have to make some changes.

This book is about optimization — about working with the finished product until you are fully satisfied that you are getting the best results from every page.

Applying Persuasion Architecture to web marketing makes everything measurable (although not all data yield useful information!). The result is a Marketing Optimization 5-Step process that enables continuous improvement.

Buyer modalities

Another great concept for understanding your customers' purchasing patterns is called Buyer Modalities. The expert on this subject is Angie Schottmuller, a great speaker on how to apply website psychology to conversion rate optimization. She discusses specific methods to use in order to understand the distinct modalities of the buyers who visit your websites. People think in different ways, and their different personalities determine the feelings they get when visiting your pages. There's a huge difference between buyers who purchase based on logic versus those who make decisions based on emotion.

There are four types of buyer-buying modalities—four ways that buyers interact with and think about your site. The four modalities are *competitive, spontaneous, methodical,* and *humanistic.* Competitive and spontaneous buyers are fast and have quick reactions while methodical and humanistic buyers are slow and somewhat unstructured.

Those comprising the competitive modality are fast, but they make structured and logic-based decisions. They ask *"What makes your solution the best?"* because *they* want to be the best. Spontaneous buyers are all about quick, unstructured, and emotion-based decisions. *Why should I choose you, right now? What are you going to do for me immediately?*

In contrast, there are the two slower buyer modalities. Methodical buyers make structured and logic-based decisions—just like the competitive group—but they take their time. They often want to know *how* your process or solution works. The humanistic bunch are also slow in making a decision, but they do it in a more unstructured and emotional way. They ask, *"Who uses your solution for my problem?"* and *"How does it relate to the individuals at hand?"*

Knowing these four buyer modalities will help you understand precisely who is visiting your site and how you need to approach them and talk to them. You have to shift your mindset and try to understand your websites in a completely different way. This is a strong basis for understanding the framework that will work for you and your business. Buyer modalities may be important to you, web analytics may be important to you, and the right qualitative data may be important to you. I'm going to show you what has proven to work for *me,* but you need to try to figure out the right system for *you*—in your own scenario, for the people visiting your websites, and for your experience.

BUYER MODALITIES CHECKLIST

COMPETITIVE Bottom line UVP , "Best" evidence, Learn/achieve challenges	✓
HUMANISTIC People/Others-focused, People photos, Stories & Reviews	✓
SPONTANEOUS Personalization, Guarantee, Time-savers/Tools, Hot trends/Urgency	✓
METHODICAL Process Steps, Factual details, Timing expectations	✓

Eisenberg, Bryan. Eisenberg, Jeffery. David, Lisa T. 2006. Persuasive Online Copywriting.

Gathering intelligence

At every step in the Marketing Optimization System, we collect and analyze data in two different ways—qualitatively and quantitatively. Analyzing qualitatively helps you to understand exactly who visits your websites and know why they should be buying products from your online store. Quantitative data is all about numbers and metrics. It is the analytics and the goals that are calculated from your marketing results.

It's one thing to gather all this insight, but the difficult part is using it in a constructive way that will result in higher sales and leads. Here, I will share tips to help you with each of the different tools. You can then apply them to our system in a way that best suits your needs.

Once you determine the things that help your websites to make more money or increase your conversion rates, you can scale those things up to increase your bottom line.

Tools and goals

Now it's time to create the right tool kit for *your* Marketing Optimization System. In this section, I'll talk about some of the different technologies you may want to use, and we'll discuss these tools in the upcoming case studies as well. What goes into the ideal tool kit for your marketing optimization plan?

I recommend a tool kit using:

- Google Analytics to measure your data
- HotJar for exit polls, heatmaps, scrolling data, and mouse tracking
- Visual Website Optimizer or Optimizely for split testing
- SurveyMonkey to gather feedback in survey format
- UserTesting to watch people go through your web pages
- Unbounce to create landing pages for paid advertising and lead generation landing pages
- LeadPages to create e-mail opt-in landing pages for Facebook Ads
- ECommerce Dashboard (WordPress, Shopify, Bigcommerce, Magento, etc.)

When you've stocked your tool pack, the following stage is to decide your objectives. You need to recognize both your quantifiable objectives and your subjective objectives. For instance, for a blog, one of your objectives may be to increment offers and remarks on your substance. In an assistance based business, your objective might be to gather leads. In eCommerce, you'll have a wide range of sorts of objectives—expanding your normal request esteem, making more profit, and expanding your transformation rates from your promoting efforts to support your general bottom line. You additionally need to enhance to improve the pick ins and manufacture your email list. You need to improve your returning customer income and increment your leads for versatile. You additionally need to decline the skip rate of your top point of arrival. This, consequently, will likewise diminish the time it takes another customer to make a first buy.

Diminishing the time to request is a significant objective for eCommerce. To do this, you need to make sense of works best for you. To do that, start by making what we call the 80-20. Most eCommerce destinations make 80% of their income off of 20% of their inventory. Ensure that you realize what that 20% is—and advance those items on your site. That way, you can get a huge number of individuals to buy more in a shorter period of time.

When you comprehend your information and realize what your objectives are, at that point you can continue to testing and analysis. Breaking the general transformation into an arrangement of steps will enable you to distinguish where all of this should lead, guiding you through a pipe to your definitive ultimate objective. Taking a gander at the 10,000 foot view will empower you to take a gander at your information—customer referrals, high traffic ricochet rate pages, high-traffic/low skip rate pages, explicit high nations—in an alternate way. Knowing where to start depends both on your information and your insight of where you can accomplish the greatest increases with the least sum of exertion. You should see how a lot of time and traffic it'll take you to accomplish statistical hugeness. In nonmathematical language, statistical hugeness reveals to you something about the degree to which your outcomes are "genuine" and delegate of your testing crowd. You need to guarantee that you run your tests for in any event a hundred changes on every variety, except the careful number may be one of a kind to your own site.

The subsequent stage is to inquire about to assemble as a lot of information—both quantitative and subjective—as conceivable before beginning the showcasing advancement process. Social occasion information is the most tedious part of the procedure since we at that point need to investigate that information to use it in an exact manner.

Qualitative insight

Utilizing subjective understanding can appear to be overwhelming, and it takes a great deal of time. Be that as it may, it's the most significant part of the whole Marketing Optimization System. Indeed, the undertakings that are generally the toughest to scale are the ones that have the greatest effect. For instance, jumping on the telephone with visitors to your site who deserted your shopping basket can take a great deal of time and exertion, yet talking legitimately to these visitors is precisely where the greatest undiscovered open doors lie.

It is here where you will realize what's happening in your potential customer's brain. You absolutely never need to make presumptions about what your visitors need. You need to ask them, give reviews, or listen to customer administration calls to comprehend why they are—or are not—buying items from your store. When you have unmistakably characterized the issues they're having and take in what is missing from your site, you would then be able to make explicit arrangements. As you find out about what is going on in your customers' brains, you can enhance your eCommerce webpage to display the copywriting, advantages, and one of a kind worth they're searching for on your eCommerce site. The best copywriting will be taken legitimately from the customers, utilizing language they comprehend, and tending to their issues—in this manner improving their lives.

There is an enthusiastic trigger in their lives that makes them head to Google and quest for an answer to their concern. After they arrive, it might take a couple touch focuses with your image to make them return and buy. Use email and retargeting promoting efforts to keep your image at the top of your potential customer's psyche. A retargeting showcasing effort is when advertisements from a webpage you visit start to show up on different sites that you visit. Potential customers will begin contrasting your image straightforwardly to whomever they think their competitors are. Considering this, you can see that it's significant to see how your customer feels about your competitors with the goal that you can obviously separate yourself.

For instance, an Internet client will visit Google and quest for a specific kind of item or for an answer to an issue they have. You need to be there to tackle their concern. You need to comprehend what they're searching for and where they may go to discover it. Your promotions need to address the particular issue. What's more, past that underlying advance, your point of arrival needs to present arrangements that will improve their lives. That is the thing that subjective information is about—building customer profiles, characterizing personas, and making perfect snap M.A.P.s, evacuating any pointless rubbing or trouble.

You likewise need to know all of the watchwords potential purchasers are searching for. Not just the watchwords they're composing into their inquiry, yet in addition those that are really driving the most profit to your site. What is your customer's plan, and what watchwords are really driving the most changes and leads?

So how would we figure this out? Understanding subjective information can be troublesome, however there are a wide range of tools you can utilize to "read" your potential customer's brain. This is known as learning the voice of the customer.

UserTesting

One of the tools I use in each undertaking is UserTesting. What different brands would they say they are tapping on? What is their client experience going to be? How are individuals really finding your site? UserTesting helps answer these inquiries. It's a pen that empowers you come to an obvious conclusion and decide how individuals are utilizing your site. It will likewise assist you with seeing why individuals are or are not finishing the checkout procedure.

You will likewise need to use UserTesting to break down your competitors. Make a list of the destinations you believe are your principle competitors and utilize the equivalent tool to watch individuals experience those locales. This will enable you to recognize what customers like or dislike about different locales, and you can utilize this information to look at to your own site. You'll be capable to characterize your customer profile better and talk to people with direct promoting messages planned for taking care of their particular issues.

HotJar

Another extraordinary tool we strongly suggest is HotJar. HotJar records recordings of your visitors as they utilize your site, permitting you to see all that they do—each mouse development, parchment, snap, and structure connection. It's free for up to a specific sum of sessions, however HotJar is an absolute necessity for each site you possess.

To get the most out of utilizing a tool like HotJar, I prescribe an every day assessment of the information. From the outset, you can disregard all the session accounts that are under three pages long. Simply watch the session accounts with the longest lengths. While seeing them, you will perceive how the visitor is perusing your site—where they go, what they're tapping on, and why they are or are not changing over to a deal or lead. It resembles getting a live quality confirmation test on your customer's adventure through your site. In the event that the visitor peruses a couple of pages, at that point proceeds onward to include something to the truck, you can see the M.A.P. that they picked to take.

For instance, when a customer visits a class explicit page originating from Google, HotJar will give you where their mouse moves, how far they scroll, and what they click on. In the event that the visitor appears to be keen on the item, they will tap on "include to truck" and afterward go to the shopping basket. Here, you will perceive how far they get into the checkout experience. In the event that they don't look at, it may provoke you to confirm that the shopping basket UI—or even the value—is causing them to forsake. This is central in helping us structure a hypothesis of where we should start to enhance. This procedure should be possible for any page on your site, and it gives extremely valuable data.

Qualaroo

Another great qualitative tool is Qualaroo. Qualaroo makes it possible to use intelligent pop-up surveys depending on different variables. For example, you can trigger a survey to a visitor based on the amount of time on page, pages visited, number of site visits, referring source, or any internal data. These interactions can be used to gather insights about visitors, address their unique needs in real time, and ultimately turn them into valuable customers.

The best place to use Qualaroo is on your cart or checkout page. A survey will pop up if the customers move their mouse toward the "back" button. In the survey, we try to determine why they aren't checking out. We want to know their intent and why they may not be buying. We also use Qualaroo on the conversion thank you page after a purchase and ask, "What made you purchase from us today?" Surveys can help you understand why people are *not* taking the action you want as well as why people *are* taking the action you want. There's no better time to engage with your actual customers than after they actually connect with you and your site in some way — whether it be on the e-mail opt-in thank you page or after the purchase confirmation.

Now that you've followed these suggestions and have your ideal customer profile, one of the key tips I can give you is to reach out to as many customers and as many people who didn't convert as possible. You want to get people on the phone — understand exactly how they found you, what their intent was before finding you, and why they did or did not convert. Talk to all of your direct ideal customers and understand exactly what their real problems are. The more you talk to people, the more you will understand your "audience" and know exactly what problems that they have, what they want and need, and how you can help serve them better in the future. The more research you do, the better off you will be.

So you may be asking, *why do all this?* Well, you do it because it really does help you to better define the personas visiting your site. Making guesses and assumptions doesn't help you achieve or improve, and it certainly doesn't help your potential customers find what they're searching for. This is so much more important than spending money on advertising. All of this qualitative data comes into play with predictive analysis. If you're able to connect the dots properly, you can almost always predict how your advertising campaigns are going to work. This insight is the secret to increasing your sales and leads in the next six months.

Marketing optimization system

Let's bring everything together into a more advanced process that I call the Marketing Optimization System. It's a five-step process to increase profit from the existing traffic of your eCommerce website. You can use what I've learned to help you make better decisions and get bigger results. There are many other tools that can be used and things that can be done, but I have included only the essential steps that I believe are needed in *every* system.

Creating the right system for you is all about gathering the qualitative and quantitative data and using that insight to obtain bigger impacts from our tests. It doesn't matter how much testing you do or how easy the testing is — *if you're not testing the right things, then you're not getting the best results possible.*

Marketing optimization takes into account web design, marketing in general, web development, web analytics, and the customers who visit your websites. Do you understand the voice of the customers who are visiting your websites? Who's your target audience? What are their pains, and what are the problems they're dealing with before they actually arrive? What queries are they entering into Google before arriving at your landing pages? These are some of the things I'll be showing you — the importance of knowing who visits your site, where they go, what they do, and what you should do with that information.

PHASE 1 -STRATEGIC EVALUATION

Your first step is to break down your target market into your ideal customers. Your ideal customer is also known as an *avatar*. Defining your customer avatar is critical. You see, most companies and retailers are not meeting their customers' needs. You need to ensure that you have a clear understanding of your customers' needs and are targeting the right audience so that you can speak to them in a language they're familiar with. The voice or language you want to use is *their* voice.

Here is where you will use the customer's mindset — it will be the foundation for the personas that are more likely to buy from your online store. You want to understand the average demographics of your ideal customers — where they live, their age range, if they have children, average household income, and where they shop online. You also want to understand the lifestyle factors of your visitors. What are their hobbies and interests? How do their emotional states affect their buying modes? In addition, you can use Google Analytics to segment the visitors based on the different browsers they're using to view your website. How many visitors are using the desktop version versus a mobile or a tablet?

> **Each time you publish content on your site, you need to keep your target audience in mind.**

PHASE 2 – 5 - STEP PROCESS

The key to a successful strategy is iterating quickly and never ceasing in the quest for improvement. Then we need to validate each hypothesis using split testing. Here is where I will walk you through the 5-Step Process of the Marketing Optimization System. Start with qualitative insight, and understand that *why*. What is actually going on in your customers' minds? Do they like your products? How can you address their concerns when they first arrive at your /product pages? If they don't purchase, can you determine what influenced that decision?

Then, create different personas for people. Build these personas to create ideal click M.A.P.s for each visitor. Learn the pains, problems, and desires of each of your ideal customers. Talk to your visitors as much as you possibly can. They will let you in on their secrets about your website. This will enable you to stop making assumptions about what you think your customers want.

Next, bring in the quantitative data to see where your customers are actually going on your site. This is all based on the 80/20 rule. You make 80% of your traffic from 20% of your pages. You break it all up into your most trafficked pages, your most trafficked pages by revenue, your highest bounce rate pages, and then your top AdWords by conversion rate.

After that, you want to separate your personas based on the research you've gathered. For example, you want to know things like:

- How many people are using your site on an old computer?
- How many visitors are browsing within a mobile experience?
- How are people really seeing your websites?
- Which Internet browsers are your customers using the most?

Don't assume your visitors are using the latest computer technology. Know their favorite browsers—Safari? Chrome? Internet Explorer? If you have a lot of people using old IE browsers, it could mean they're in schools or government agencies, and that will define your demographic. It's a very important part of building your persona.

You may also want to document your business goals and see what is most important to the business stakeholders. Then can prioritize the ROI for each of the individual tests. For eCommerce, we need to define not only conversion goals and success metrics, but also the micro-goals that led up to the sale. For example, how many people clicked the "add to cart" button? Which individuals are playing a site video before they buy? What are your cart abandonment rates?

From all of this, you can create a hypothesis—an educated guess.

Every website out there is unique. That's why I recommend going through this process:

- Understand your qualitative data
- Understand your quantitative data
- Create a hypothesis
- Establish your personas with a unique value proposition

- Win quickly, scaling those wins to really improve your bottom line

This is the basic routine that we will go through for the five-step process in the Marketing Optimization System. It's all about that discovery process—creating a hypothesis, executing and creating tests, reviewing the analytics, and then scaling and growing over time.

You want to understand your customers and their problems. You want to create products to solve those problems, and you want to scale what works to improve your goals with short-term wins.

STEP 1 – DISCOVERY

The secret to running successful split tests is doing a lot of research. We review quantitative and qualitative data to determine where we can find the biggest opportunities. Then we prioritize the changes we ere going to make.

During this process, we establish what we can optimize immediately to get our quick wins using quantitative data. We do Google Analytics audits to review our top goals and our top landing pages, and we do revenue tracking, conversion tracking, and heatmap tracking.

We also utilize qualitative analysis. Understanding qualitative data helps us find some of the pains, problems, and desires of our ideal customers. This, in turn, enables us to find more opportunities to increase our overall eCommerce sales. The tools to do this used to be expensive and complicated to use. But now, great tools like UserTesting.com—where you can watch users/visitors travel through your site to understand exactly what's going on—are simple and readily available to anyone. UserTesting will help you understand how people are traveling through your websites, and you can break things down into a summary of what you've learned from the data. This will help you build out your wireframes based on insight and design feedback from those specific tests.

We'll also use heatmap software, Visual Website Optimizer, HotJar, or Inspectlet to see specifically where people are clicking and tools like Survey Monkey to review specific feedback customers and potential customers give us. As mentioned before, the survey can be added to many areas of your websites to automate the collection of qualitative feedback. Another tool that we'll use is Qualaroo to create a survey page that allows us to collect data from people who are leaving the website.

STEP 2 – HYPOTHESIS

Once we know where we need to start testing, we want to create a hypothesis. We'll use data and facts to come up with specific educated guesses. Then we'll outline an experiment to test the hypothesis and discuss how the results might impact the website. Creating a hypothesis is very important because not only do you want to be able to track what is going on and measure properly, you also want to understand how it relates to each part of your business—how it affects your stakeholders, different business managers, and clients. After that, you need to figure out which of these different tasks takes priority.

Prioritizing can be done in different ways. I use a process created by Bryan Eisenberg. His approach encourages you to dig into the human element rather than looking at visitor feedback as qualitative data. In the planning mode, Bryan encourages you to answer these questions before running a test:

- Who are you trying to persuade?
- What action do you want them to take?
- What action do they want to take?

ConversionXL.com broke Bryan's process down into an easy to understand format:
Measure.
 Design the test and define its parameters for success. Bryan recommends asking three more questions:

- What action do you want them to take, and where do we measure it?
- What pages do we want them to test?
- Where/how do we track success?

For example, you may have noticed in the past that many existing customers signed up because of the videos they have watched on your site. The goal of your pages may indeed be to get people to watch a specific video. So you set up a specific tracking to see if they're watching it or not. To get more people to watch it, you might try testing the video's actual thumbnail. You judge your success on whether or not you're converting from those who watch the video.
Improve.
 Once you have the data, your next step is to improve on it. For example, if there are more people watching the video and converting, what does the video have that the page does not? If that "aha!" moment in the video is due to a testimonial or a success guarantee, is that specific information properly reflected on the page to encourage non-video watchers, too? Now that you have the data, learn from it and make improvements.

Prioritizing.
How many hours — development hours and man hours — will be necessary for this test to have an impact?
Impact.
This is the amount of time or the reduced cost that would change the event or produce a successful test. Are you increasing on the whole customer base or just a segment of it? Are you looking for a 1% or a 20% increase?
Resources.
What is the cost of the tools, people, and everything else associated with running the actual test? How much will the actual test cost?

The strategy of creating a hypothesis is taken from the scientific method. I have adapted Bryan Eisenberg's approach, combining it with a traditional hypotheses framework, to determine how to best organize each experiment idea.

Hypothesis Framework

A good hypothesis framework contains the following elements:

- *Description of the observation to be explained*

    a. Who are you trying to persuade?

    b. What action do you want them to take?

    c. What action do they want to take?

- *Description of the process hypothesized to cause the observation*

    a. What relevant observations are explained?

    b. What relevant observations are not explained?

    c. What observations are incompatible with the explanation?

- *Description of how you will track success for the experiment*

    a. What goals and metrics are tracked during this experiment?

    b. If the hypothesis is validated, how would it affect the bottom line?

    c. What is the estimate for minimal success?

-

STEP 3 – EXECUTION

First, you discovered your ideal target audience and defined who was visiting your website, and then you created a hypothesis for each experiment. Now you are going to develop the creative for the different variations in each experiment and set up the split testing using software like Visual Website Optimizer or Optimizely.

This is one of the most time-consuming sections of the process. Sometimes it can require a few different people to accomplish all the tasks needed. For example, when we're ready to create the mockups for the split testing variations, I develop wireframes for each variation. A wireframe is simply a black-and-white skeleton of a web page. The wireframes are turned into color designs using Photoshop. Once the color design is perfect, we can code the HTML needed to create the web pages. Then we can set up the split test directly in the testing software.

The experiments are added to the testing software and then set up to track a few main goals. The main goals that I usually set up for all tests include:

- Conversions – track visits to "Thank You" confirmation page
- Revenue – track revenue on each visit to "Thank You" confirmation page
- Clicks – track engagement with the page variation

After doing quality assurance testing of the experiments in all the necessary browsers, we will then begin the testing process for a specific segment of traffic. For example, if we're testing a product page from paid advertising, we will run tests for a desktop website differently than mobile-specific traffic.

Sometimes a test succeeds, and other times it fails. But it's important to analyze each success and failure in order to learn from them.

STEP 4 – REVIEW

After the tests are successful, we need to be sure that it makes sense to release the new creation on the live site as the new baseline control. We will use a website data analyst to run statistics to check that the new changes are going help our conversion rates. Just because a split test wins doesn't always mean you make more money.

Not only do we need to review the data from the finished test, but we also need to determine if the winner will truly help the bottom line growth of the business. There are many factors to consider. How difficult will it be to implement into the production website? What if the winner only corresponds to a specific segment of traffic? We should test all segments to ensure it produces the same results for all visitors on any device they may be using.

STEP 5 – SCALE

We're ready now to really grow our business and make more money. Once we determine what tests are helping to improve our conversion rates, increase sales, and generate more leads, we can then take what we learned and apply it to other areas of the eCommerce store. For example, if we learn that a new landing page headline helps increase conversion by 20 percent, we can then take that headline and create PPC ads with it. We can also test that high-converting headline on our homepage or category pages. This is how we scale all successful experiments.

PHASE 3 - BOTTOM LINE GROWTH PLAN

Just because a test wins for a specific segment of your website traffic doesn't mean it will win for every visitor coming to your website. That's why each test needs to be analyzed on a case-by-case basis. The average eCommerce website has five major templates:

- Homepage
- Category page
- Product page
- Contact page
- Customer service pages like FAQ or return policy

There's also the shopping cart page and the checkout process. These are the major sections of the eCommerce site that determine the whole structure.

We test the highest traffic and most popular product pages on a small business eCommerce website. When we know that we have a new winning version, we can implement the successful elements into the default product templates. That way, all of the product pages now have the best converting elements across the entire website. This is how you take one winning page and scale it to grow your bottom line. The strategy can also work for your category templates, landing pages, campaign-specific microsites, and external websites.

AFFILIATE MARKETING
What Affiliate Marketing is all about

Affiliate Marketing is a fantastic way for Internet-savvy entrepreneurs to make money on the Web. While the possibilities for making money online are endless, affiliate marketing is one of the most dynamic ways to do so. Unlike many endeavors, affiliate marketing gives everyone an equal opportunity to make money with their passions. Sports car enthusiasts, gardeners, and video-game connoisseurs can all try their hand at affiliate marketing, learn what works and what does not, and earn an income promoting things they enjoy. If you have the patience and dedication to build a well-constructed site, affiliate marketing can help you build a thriving part-time or full-time business doing what you love.

There are numerous ways to integrate affiliate links into your online content, such as linking a picture of a product on your blog to an online store where a user can buy that product, showing actual items for sale that are related to your content, or even just integrating a banner ad or text links. When used effectively, affiliate marketing can help you make ads feel less like advertising and more like content, improving the experience for your users. Because affiliate compensation is linked to the sales and leads that you drive for your advertisers, you also have the potential to earn more money than you could with banner or paid search ads.

If you are considering becoming an affiliate, The Complete Guide to Affiliate Marketing on the Web is a very good place to start. The book goes into detail about selecting programs that are right for you, the importance of generating unique and quality content, and attracting customers that will earn you a return. It includes common mistakes and interviews with successful affiliates, who offer many tips and tricks that they have learned along the way.

If you are an online retailer or are looking to drive more traffic to your own site, this book also offers step-by-step guidance for setting up an affiliate program to attract new customers. By following these guidelines, business owners can increase revenues and grow their businesses by essentially recruiting a network of marketers to help promote their products.

At eBay, for example, there are more than 100,000 affiliates that promote eBay products across the Web, driving a significant amount of traffic to eBay sites around the world. Our affiliates are a very important part of our online marketing efforts. eBay pays its affiliates a percentage of the revenue we make from that traffic in return and works closely with affiliates to ensure they are maximizing the effectiveness of their advertising space and driving quality traffic to eBay. Because these affiliates are driving traffic to eBay that the company might not have otherwise attracted, the result is a win-win for eBay and for its affiliates.

One of the things we have learned at eBay is that the most successful affiliates provide trustworthy, engaging sites for their visitors that include unique content and relevant affiliate offers. This ensures that the customers driven through the affiliate to the merchant site are interested in the products the affiliate is promoting and are, therefore, more likely to make a purchase. Engaged customers, as we call them, are much more profitable for both the affiliate and the business for which the affiliate is driving traffic. The Complete Guide will give you a very good set of basics on how to become a productive affiliate.

A few other tips to consider for driving good traffic include:

• Offer customers timely, relevant content and promote affiliate offers that will help customers solve a particular problem. This will make your site more valuable and ensure your customers come back to you.
• Know the products you are promoting and do not offer customers too many things at once. You will attract quality traffic by providing fewer, more trustworthy recommendations.
• Where possible, work closely with the merchants you are promoting to figure out what works best for them. It is likely they will have insights that will help you and your campaigns.
• It may sounds obvious, but read the terms and conditions from the merchants you want to work with. This is the Merchants' way of telling you how they want you to promote their program. They all have different rules and this may help you determine who you really want to work with. It can also help you avoid getting expired from their programs by employing tactics that are not allowed in their terms.
• Test, test, test is a mantra to live by in affiliate marketing. Try different layouts and copy, determine what works and fine-tune your campaign to maximize efficiency and profits. What works will be different for different types of affiliates, different products and merchants, so it is crucial for all affiliates to experiment and fine-tune.
Success in affiliate marketing, as with anything else, requires patience and a continued effort to learn and adapt to what works. Whether you are launching an affiliate program or an affiliate marketing campaign, The Complete Guide to Affiliate Marketing on the Web is a great place to start your ongoing education. With this book and a healthy dose of entrepreneurial energy and creativity, you will be well on your way to success. When you think about affiliate marketing, there are two main ideas you need to understand. Your perspective on these ideas will drive how you deploy affiliate marketing for your Web site or business.

Affiliate Marketing Options

Essentially, you have two affiliate marketing options.

• Host an offshoot program on your Web website so others can join your subsidiary system and sell your items on their Web locales. They will procure a commission for every deal, and you will sell more items through them. This is a definitive answer for the individuals who have items to sell — envision your items advertised for nothing on thousands of Web locales over the world.

• Join an offshoot system and sell different items on your Web webpage for which you will win a commission on every deal. You don't do anything and pay nothing. The arrangement is basic — everything you do is keep the substance refreshed with what you need to advertise on your Web website, and money the month to month commission check.

My first genuine presentation to offshoot advertising was through experimentation. I put an advertisement on my Web website and trusted that somebody would tap on it, make a buy, and in the long run, I would get a commission from that deal. This was not a productive endeavor, and eventually, I expelled the standard advertisements from my site. It didn't work because fundamentally due to a need of promoting — viably displaying the items on my Web webpage — and the specialized impediments of how the member showcasing program was sent.

Establishing a partner showcasing program of your own or going along with another person's subsidiary program will, in itself, not produce generous income for you except if you adequately convey and administer it. Following this brief presentation we will get into the subtleties of how to establish your very own partner program or join an associate system and guarantee that you are ideally situated for progress.

Consider the essential way of thinking and standards of a partner advertising program: You can sell others' items on your Web website for nothing, and they pay you a commission to do it. You absolutely never touch the items; are not answerable for the deal, bundling, shipping, customer administration, customer protests, issue goals, returns, or cerebral pains; and for the straightforward demonstration of permitting their items to be sold on your Web website, you get a month to month commission check.

On the other hand, in the event that you wish to establish your very own associate promoting effort for your items, you are actualizing a program that permits others to sell your items for you, and you pay them a commission expense. Rather of your items being sold on your Web website, they can be sold on handfuls, hundreds, or thousands of other high-traffic destinations. The expanded deals and profits more than offset the commission charges you will pay, regardless you have full authority over the members, can affirm who is permitted to take an interest in your program, and still hold administrative control overs your items, estimating, inventory, deals, and record keeping.

Partner advertising furnishes you with a minimal effort or no-cost arrangement to advance your items and produce income. With practically zero speculation and expanded deals and income, for what reason would you not need to grasp offshoot promoting? In the event that you are the proprietor, proprietor, or chief of a customary block and cement or online business, offshoot promoting on the Web can open entryways you never envisioned in wording of deals volume and expanded profits. Partner promoting can spare you thousands of dollars in costs contrasted and customary advertising projects, and arrive at business sectors at no other time conceivable through selling your items on other Web destinations. In the event that you are not up to the test of beginning your own subsidiary showcasing program, joining a member arrange is a brisk and simple way to start producing income for your business. Remember that you needn't bother with to be a specialist in offshoot advertising to be exceptionally effective. We should start our partner advertising experience!

Affiliate Marketing Principles

Subsidiary showcasing has absolutely developed in the previous decade and has detonated in both ubiquity and profitability. It has extended into each viewpoint of the Web and has the potential to be one of the more rewarding ways of creating the two deals and income. The fundamental standards of associate showcasing are sound and have stood the test of time: You advance my stuff on your Web webpage and I will pay you a commission for every deal, or I will advance your stuff on my Web website and you pay me a commission for every deal. Any business interface on any Web webpage is tied to member or pay-per-click (PCP) advertising in some structure or another.

There is no item available to be purchased anyplace that is not part of an associate system. On the off chance that you need to purchase golf hardware, automotive parts, running shoes, books, motion pictures, CDs, electronic gear, PCs, and so on, somebody has a subsidiary program you can join. Whenever executed appropriately there is no explanation behind member showcasing not to be a gigantic achievement. I will give you one last alert, however: I don't buy in to or accept the cases that, "I joined a zillion partner programs, put a pack of advertisements on my Web destinations, and now everything I do is sit back drinking my frosted tea on the sea shore in front of my million-dollar sea see house in Florida watching the mail bearer convey fists full of commission checks to me." If it were this worthwhile we would all be on the sea shore tallying our profits. The point is that it tends to be truly profitable, and on the off chance that you execute your very own offshoot program, you can significantly build your item deals volume.

Ideally you presently have a decent understanding of subsidiary showcasing. The accompanying is a recap of the two essential offshoot promoting techniques.

• Joining an Affiliate Program or Network: This implies that you have your own Web website and that you join a subsidiary program or system selling different items. For instance, you have a Web webpage or blog about running. To increment your income you join the associate system of an enormous running shoe shipper. This is free to you, and in the wake of going along with, they give you the data to include their items to your Web webpage. They will give you exceptional URLs which particularly recognize the deals that started from your Web webpage. You can energize your webpage visitors to purchase the showing shoes to following the picture and other data you set on your Web website. At the point when they click on the picture, they are taken to the shipper's site — normally straightforwardly to the item they need to purchase — where they can put in the request. When the request is handled and finished, you are told of the deal and of your commission sum. You approach to an online record to monitor your statistics, income, and other indispensable data. You can change items as often as you need to keep your Web webpage consistently changing and intriguing. You don't process the deal, handle or ship the merchandise, give customer administration, or whatever else. When the exchange is finished, you have earned your commission. The shipper must wrap up!

• Create or Manage Your Own In-House Affiliate Program: This implies you have your own Web website and items to sell. You need to extend your commercial center past your Web website and utilize the power of thousands of different destinations to advance and sell your items for you. The individuals who advance these items for you on their Web destinations are your subsidiaries, and they fall into the classification above. They place your items and materials on their Web webpage. On the off chance that somebody visits their webpage and taps on your items, an extraordinary member connect takes them to your Web website where you complete the exchange. You presently have the extravagance of highlighting and advancing your items on Web destinations everywhere throughout the world at no expense to you; arriving at millions of individuals you couldn't have recently come to and who might not have thought about you or your items. As every deal is finished, the subsidiary acquires a commission. You may think about whether this implies you will gain less profit on the grounds that you are paying 10 percent or more for every deal to another person. That is genuine, however hypothetically, you are selling essentially a bigger number of items than you would have previously; presently, you are advancing your items on hundreds or thousands of significant Web destinations. You should keep up your offshoot account status, produce month to month checks, and administer your partners endorsements, account upkeep, etc; so there is some overhead and work on your part, however commonly, it is negligible. As you include new items to your inventory, you include them to your associate program, and your offshoots in a flash start advancing them. You at that point procedure the deal, handle and ship the merchandise, give customer administration, handle the exchanges, and some other fundamental subtleties.

There are a few decisions of associate promoting software accessible to you in the event that you wish to manufacture your very own member arrange or introduce an offshoot program on your Web webpage. We will cover these in detail in later sections, yet here are your general choices:

• Affiliate Network: In this case the software is gave and facilitated by the partner organize supplier. You just join the existing system and offer your items available to be purchased to different individuals of the associate system. They handle the program administration, announcing, commission installments, and the sky is the limit from there.

• Hosted Affiliate Network Software: The software is not gave to you or introduced on your Web server. The software supplier has it on their servers, and you pay a charge, generally month to month, for help and upkeep. All you have on your Web webpage is a little piece of following code; your work is insignificant. Since they claim and host the software you immediately advantage from software overhauls, patches, and upgrades; in addition, they are answerable for every one of the servers, reinforcements, and unwavering quality. Furthermore, specialized help is included with the bundle.

• Affiliate Network Software (Stand-Alone): You purchase the software bundle and claim the permit to use it as you see fit. This is a one-time charge and it tends to be costly. You introduce the software on your Web server and coordinate it with your shopping basket or inventory the executives framework; once in a while establishment is included for nothing or for a little charge. This software is pressed with highlights, and there are no repetitive charges except if you need to pursue overhauls and fixes, or other help which is normally constrained or excluded.

The least complex and most foolproof way of drawing in rush hour gridlock to your Web webpage would be to print the Web website's name and URL on your T-shirt, thump on each entryway in your neighborhood, and offer to pay every individual a dollar to enter your webpage. This is not realistic, of course, in spite of the fact that the idea of member promoting is very little extraordinary. In the first place, this method is work concentrated. Second, you would turn into your local's most noticeably awful bad dream. What's more, third, you can just reach such a large number of houses in a solitary day. At last, you would discover pretty much nothing if any expansion in Web webpage traffic. This speculative situation teaches us, in any case, about the nuts and bolts of producing traffic through a partner arrange. Straightforward is not continually going to be simple or successful, and you just have a constrained sum of time and cash at your disposal to accomplish this task. The sum of traffic got per unit of time or cash consumed ought to be as high as could be expected under the circumstances and traffic-creating methods ought to be lingering. Remaining traffic implies that it will proceed to produce traffic moving along without any more venture of time or cash long after the mechanism has been set into place. Its inverse is what I call flashflood traffic systems; these strategies produce traffic increments for a brief period of time, normally, just while you are contributing cash into it, with no genuine promise of repeating traffic.

Let me give both of you models which will obviously give you how the two kinds of traffic contrast.

• Imagine that you just purchased a changeless connection on a blogroll; the assortment of interfaces generally found on the correct side of a blog. The sum of traffic you get relies upon the notoriety of the blog, of course, yet the traffic will proceed for a considerable length of time, if not years, and the connection will stand out from web indexes. This is a model of a leftover traffic system.

• An alternate situation is that you post a topical article on your blog, and before you know it, your servers can scarcely keep up; the story made it over the blogosphere. After seven days, in any case, the traffic from the blog has come to a pounding end. This is an extraordinary model of flashflood traffic. Paying for traffic through Google AdWords is another flashflood traffic procedure. At the point when you stop paying, the traffic stops. The accompanying list features factors engaged with traffic the board.

• What is the sum of time or cash required?

• What sum of traffic will you acquire per unit of time or cash?

• What type of traffic, leftover or flashflood, does the procedure produce?

• Are there any shrouded advantages or issues?

It is significant to perceive that driving traffic to your Web webpage is basic to the achievement of a member program. A partner program lets you expand your Web webpage and additionally item visibility all through other Web destinations advancing your items and driving that customer traffic to your website. As a byproduct of this traffic and coming about deal/transformation, you pay a commission to the referrer/partners.

The world of associate traffic is full of misconceptions. Here are a few actualities and substances of partner promoting.

• Setting up a successful offshoot traffic program is not really simple and will take a speculation of time and cash, yet it can return enormous profits.

• Affiliate promoting doesn't automatically mean a gigantic increment in Web webpage traffic. Setting up or joining a partner program or system alone won't really get you any recognizable increment traffic. Despite everything you will have to advance your program through different methods all together to make it powerful.

• You should maintain a strategic distance from publicity and assemble believability in your Web website and your items.

• Some Web surfers are hesitant to click an offshoot connection or standard; yet many member programs have worked in strategies to help battle this. Everything returns to believability; on the off chance that they trust you, this is a non-issue.

In conventional associate promoting, the traffic produced is just a side issue and the principle center is around the marketing projection; the traffic may be generally low, yet the transformation to deals can be fabulous.

Projects that empower clients to just buy in to a pamphlet or pursue a network or gathering are not expected to promptly create deals. These activities are not viewed as a section of associate showcasing, yet part of a compensation for each activity (PPA) crusade.

Subsidiary traffic is fit to those cases who look for an immediate transformation of traffic to deals. There are different sides to this story. You may be keen on either turning into an offshoot or selling your item through a member program. The principal case doesn't generally concern traffic age, however it is certainly a issue you should be acquainted with all together to make your associate program really work; or, in the event that you are keen on turning into a partner, the issue becomes boosting the income of your traffic. At the point when you approach associate showcasing, you should inquire as to whether you would purchase the item you are advancing. This is a key inquiry in light of the fact that the appropriate response is often no. For what reason would you not purchase the item? Is it of low quality? Is the language utilized to advance it too full of publicity? Do you have a repugnance toward the configuration where the offer is accessible? Okay have an issue purchasing an item from a go between and not the producer of the item? These inquiries hold the key to an increasingly powerful type of partner advertising. Analyze every issue each in turn.

Picking the Right Product

The best affiliate product to sell is the one you are most familiar with. Anything can be sold if it fits a niche, and although the niche itself might be small, the competition also will be smaller. If you have expertise in a certain field, and you pick a product related to that field, you will have a huge advantage over your competition because you will be able to understand your customers. You also will be able to instantly differentiate a quality product from a low-quality product, and quality counts. As time goes on and you attract more traffic, you build up a portfolio of affiliate products to sell to your existing customers. The basic idea is to find a customer niche you understand and know how to cater to and concentrate on marketing those products through your affiliate program.

Effective Product Web Copy or Sales Material

There are many approaches available to sell products on the Web. Why are people browsing the Web? A consistent percentage are indeed out there looking for a solution to a problem or simply looking for a product to purchase, but most of them are only looking for general information or human interaction. You should cater to those looking for a solution to a problem or a product to purchase. Catering to a small community with a high likelihood of purchase with products you know very well is a key to affiliate success. Trying to cater to everyone without specialization is much less successful. Target your Web copy to your products and provide detailed information, advantages, and reviews to generate interest. Generic banner ads plastered all over your Web site without anything else to support them will not generate conversions.

The Sales Letter Style of Web Copy

The sales letter has both advantages and disadvantages. Its use is most effective when selling products that target a niche audience. Long sales letters tend to be more effective with people 23-25 years or older and less effective with the younger ones. The sales letter format is a very old advertising and marketing approach, and its transition to the online format carries with it the advertising culture that created it. Younger people are less accustomed to the direct mail type of advertising culture and will be less likely to react to it.

Advantages of the Sales Letter Web Copy Approach:

• Less distraction to the Web reader. The sales pitch is all there is, and as the reader progresses through it, no immediate exit points can be found on the page. If someone actually reads it, the only choice faced will be whether or not to buy, which greatly increases the conversion ratio.

• The SEO effort is only directed at a single page.

• It takes relatively little time to develop.

Disadvantages of the Sale Letter Web Copy Approach:

• Many people really don't want to read a sales pitch.

• You can only target the keywords in the copy for Search Engine Optimization purposes; although, this is actually an advantage for Organic Search Engine Optimization.

• The format limits further development, because your site is essentially a sales pitch for one product.

Generalized Web Copy Sales Approach

The generalized Web copy sales approach is either a static site containing some articles or reviews about a product, or with Web 2.0, it can be a variety of formats for which you can choose the content. At the core of all this design is the desire to generate a more interactive experience. Through the use of blogs, forums, interactive flash Web designs, or social networking, the ultimate purpose is the same. Here are some tips:

• Make sure your Web site has loads of content. Not all pages need to have affiliate links in them, but all should have interesting and relevant content.

• Put in a variety of content to include industry news, Web site features, product reviews, cover stories, how to guides, new product releases, and more.

This sounds like a lot of work for selling only one product. You can sell a whole array of products on your site through your affiliate program, but I do recommend you start out small and make sure the products are somehow linked to each other and to your area of expertise; computer monitors and makeup do not really don't belong together.

The total number of pages is another advantage to successful Web sites compared to sales letter Web sites. This is an extremely important factor when it comes to search engine optimization. What you need to keep in mind now is that the more pages in a Web site the better. You cannot achieve that with a traditional sales letter.

CPSIA information can be obtained
at www.ICGtesting.com
Printed in the USA
LVHW060759090922
727942LV00005B/187

9 781804 344187